We Will
Not Be
SILENCED

D1412404

WORKBOOK

We Will
Not Be
SILENCED

Erwin W. Lutzer

HARVEST HOUSE PUBLISHERS
EUGENE, OREGON

Cover design by Studio Gearbox

Cover photo © imagehub / Shutterstock

Interior design by Rockwell Davis

For bulk, special sales, or ministry purchases, please call-800-547-8979. Email: Customerservice@hhpbooks.com

Ⓜ is a federally registered trademark of the Hawkins Children's LLC. Harvest House Publishers, Inc., is the exclusive licensee of the trademark.

We Will Not Be Silenced Workbook
Copyright © 2021 by Erwin W. Lutzer
Published by Harvest House Publishers
Eugene, Oregon 97408
www.harvesthousepublishers.com

ISBN 978-0-7369-8555-0 (pbk.)
ISBN 978-0-7369-8556-7 (eBook)

Printed in the United States of America

21 22 23 24 25 26 27 28 29 / CM / 10 9 8 7 6 5 4 3 2 1

*"If anyone would come after me, let him deny
himself and take up his cross and follow me.
For whoever would save his life will lose it,
but whosoever loses his life for my sake will find it."*

MATTHEW 16:24-25

Contents

How to Use This Workbook

This workbook is divided into four parts. Part 1 provides further study and application of the contents of the book *We Will Not Be Silenced*. In addition to answering questions and exploring Bible verses that will help increase your understanding of today's cultural issues, each lesson provides opportunity for you to consider how to put your learning into action, and how to more actively pray about what you've learned.

Part 2, "How Should We View Our Place in Today's Culture?," considers the role that we as Christians have in society. Here, you'll gain a clearer perspective on where we as believers stand in relationship to the government, politics, and cultural issues.

Part 3, "Preparing Ourselves to Engage with Culture," looks at how we can personally equip ourselves so that we are effective as we take a stand for truth and the gospel. There are certain characteristics we must possess in our lives to ensure we are able to remain strong in the face of cultural influences rather than succumb to them.

And Part 4 provides an overview of the main questions that have been asked by media interviewers in response to *We Will Not Be Silenced*. The answers are designed to help explain some of the reasoning behind the secular worldviews that are challenging society today, and to further enable us to respond biblically.

PART 1

We Will Not Be Silenced
Workbook

LESSON 1

How We Got Here

> The secular left does not believe that America can be fixed; they say it must be destroyed.
>
> On the rubble of America's Judeo-Christian past a new America will emerge, which they say will be free of poverty, racism, and white supremacy. The secular left's goal is a future in which everyone will be equal on their terms and the disparities of the past will be read about only in history books. Those who resist this utopian vision are to be vilified, bullied, and shamed until they admit to the mistakes of the past and embrace the secular left's great hope for the future.
>
> *We Will Not Be Silenced*, page 19

As we look at the changes taking place in culture today, we can easily come to the conclusion that things are "just happening"—that, in general, moral values are decaying and because we live in a fallen world, people will follow the sinful desires of their hearts. We may think the many problems in society are simply a range of random occurrences that don't necessarily have any connection with each other.

But if we look carefully, we'll discover that in a lot of ways, it is possible for us to connect the dots. Much of the cultural disruption occurring all around us is part of a deliberate plan, an intentional strategy to undermine the foundational pillars of society. One of those key pillars is the family.

Scripture tells us that God created the family as the very first building block of society. The Lord brought together Adam and Eve in marriage, and they had children. That happened before any other building block of society came into existence, including the government and the church.

There's a reason God made the family unit first. It is within the safe and caring confines of a family that children can receive the loving instruction of parents who give them spiritual and moral guidance in accordance with how God desires for people to live. Among the earliest instructions God gave to His people in the Old Testament had to do with *how* parenting was to be done: "These words that I command you today shall be on your heart. You shall teach them diligently to your children, and shall talk of them when you sit in your house, and when you walk by the way, and when you lie down, and when you rise" (Deuteronomy 6:6-7).

A strong society begins with a strong family. As parents raise their children in the ways of the Lord, their offspring will possess the spiritual and moral values that enable them to have a positive influence in every area of life outside of the family—including in the church and the public square.

But when the family unit falls apart or is destroyed, there is a detrimental effect on society. Much of what we see happening in today's culture is part of a carefully planned attack against the family. God's design for the family calls for specific roles for each member and puts the family before all the other units of society. The secular left believes this design stands in the way of creating a better world—one where there is more equality and justice as the secular left defines them, and not God. That is why, in their view, the family must be torn down.

Cultural Marxism's Growing Shadow

> Leading these attacks against traditional American values is a form of Marxism that is widely taught in many universities and assumed by elitists as the theory that best explains the inequalities of our society and our best hope for curing them.
>
> *We Will Not Be Silenced*, page 21

What does cultural Marxism promise that makes it look so appealing?

What are the five cultural institutions that cultural Marxists seek to capture?

The Destruction of the Nuclear Family

What did Karl Marx say families based on Judeo-Christian values do?

Why is the nuclear family said to be an obstacle to the implementation of Marxism?

What do Marxists say the Bible's teachings about marriage is the source of?

What do Marxists say is the key to liberating the family?

Why do Marxists believe the education of children should be taken out of the hands of parents and surrendered to the state?

What kind of government dependency does Marxism seek to create?

In contrast to what cultural Marxists say about the family, what do the following Bible passages teach? That is, who should have the primary responsibility of raising and training children?

Genesis 1:27-28—

Deuteronomy 6:4-7—

Proverbs 1:8—

Ephesians 6:1-4—

What are some of the secular pressures that challenge Christian families today?

Oppression Is the Key to History

Why is convincing people of their victimhood so important for cultural Marxism?

On page 25 of *We Will Not Be Silenced*, we read, "Please understand that Marx was right in pointing out that oppression exists, often in horrible ways. But his solutions are entirely wrongheaded and destructive. By locating the problem as only the external systemic oppression between classes and by ignoring the biblical doctrine of original sin and individual responsibility, he sent his followers on a path of endless and unresolved conflict."

What do the following Bible passages tell us about the source and nature of humanity's problems?

Jeremiah 17:9—

Matthew 5:18-20—

Romans 3:10-12—

Read Romans 5:19 and 6:23. Is it possible for humanity to resolve its sin problem apart from Christ?

What can we learn from the Bible about equality in Galatians 3:26-29?

What do the following passages say about meeting our own needs versus meeting other people's needs?

Matthew 20:25-28—

Romans 12:10—

1 Corinthians 10:24—

Philippians 2:3-4—

What can we learn from the following verses about God's kind of justice?

Psalm 37:27-29—

Psalm 106:3—

Micah 6:8—

Zechariah 7:9—

In what ways do you see today's cultural definition of justice being at odds with God's definition of justice?

The Benefits of the Women's Movement

On page 30 of *We Will Not Be Silenced*, we read, "The Bible teaches that the genders are equal in value but different in roles." In contrast, secular culture states that men and women are alike in every way. This latter kind of equality strives to completely erase gender distinctives and claim that the roles and aptitudes of men and women are interchangeable.

What are some ways that we see God's created distinctiveness between men and women, both in Scripture and in everyday life?

The Media: Leading the Culture

On pages 30-31 of *We Will Not Be Silenced*, we read, "We should not be surprised that the focus of the cultural Marxist revolution would center on sex and gender and race. After all, these themes play dominant roles in our lives and are especially impressionable on young people…if the biblical teaching about marriage can be redefined, then the social order can be transformed."

What are some examples of how today's media is undermining or redefining matters related to marriage, sex, gender, and race?

What are some positive ways that we, as Christians, can truthfully and lovingly uphold God's standards for marriage, sex, gender, and race before a watching world?

The Ominous Choice We Face

On page 33 of *We Will Not Be Silenced*, we read, "Secularists are not content to 'live and let live.' They are not satisfied with pluralism and the exchange of ideas. They seek not just to be equal but to dominate. That which was at one time condemned must not simply be tolerated, it must be celebrated. And that which was at one time celebrated must be condemned…Their goal is the total capitulation of the culture to *their* point of view. Dissenting voices are shamed into either submission or silence."

What are some Christian values you've felt pressured to be silent about?

What are some of the consequences we face, as Christians, for taking a stand for biblical truth and views?

With regard to persevering under cultural pressures, what encouragement can we receive from the following passages?

Matthew 5:11-12—

John 16:33—

1 Peter 3:14-17—

The Silent Church

On page 35 of *We Will Not Be Silenced*, we read, "There is another reason we have been silent. We want to be nice, welcoming, and grace-centered. We want to present Jesus as Savior to the greatest number of people possible. If what we say and believe about the secular left's agenda becomes public, we will be called haters, grace-deniers, and legalistic. We will be scrutinized with even the smallest offenses magnified. We cannot shout as loudly as the radicals, nor should we. So we retreat into silence."

As we consider how to best respond to the pressures of secular culture, what should we *not* do?

Based on the example of Jehoshaphat in 2 Chronicles 20:12, when we don't know what to do, what should be our first response?

In what ways do you think we benefit from turning our eyes upon God when we are faced with a threat?

The Purpose of This Book

On page 36 of *We Will Not Be Silenced*, we read, "I write not so much to reclaim the culture as *to reclaim the church*."

In what ways do we see the church being more influenced by the culture than the culture is by the church?

What are some simple and practical ways we can make the church attractive to secular culture without giving in to that same culture?

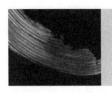

IN YOUR OWN WORDS

In 25 to 50 words, write your responses to the following questions.

What aspect of this book chapter and workbook lesson "How We Got Here" had the greatest impact on you?

How do you see this affecting the way you think and live as a Christian?

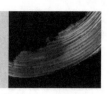
The family is under attack today as never before—and it is one of the major pillars to a strong society. Destroy the family, and society crumbles. What two or three commitments can you make in your own life to uphold biblical family values?

What are some practical ways a church can help uphold and protect the family? In the answers you write, do you see an action you can commit to right now and make a part of your service to the families in your church?

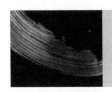

COMMITTING YOURSELF TO PRAYER

Upon completing this lesson, what five things do you desire to make a matter of prayer right now? List them here.

1.

2.

3.

4.

5.

Take a few moments now to lift these concerns up to the Lord.

The Lord is my light and my salvation;
Whom shall I fear?
The Lord is the stronghold of my life;
Of whom shall I be afraid?

Psalm 27:1

LESSON 2

Rewrite the Past
to Control the Future

In his book *1984*, Orwell described the "Ministry of Truth," whose duty it was to make the past consistent with the present. Winston Smith's assignment was to make the truth look like a lie and vice versa. If Big Brother made a prediction that didn't come to pass, the past was to be rewritten to harmonize with whatever Big Brother had said.

The point to be made is that when revolutionaries want to remake a country, they vilify the past to give legitimacy to their vision of the future. It is obvious that the "Ministry of Truth" is busily at work transforming America by rewriting the past. They say their purpose is "to root out racism," but a look at what they're doing reveals a much more sinister goal. They are using racism to attack America at its core. It's not about making America better; it's about destroying the past to build America on an entirely different foundation.

We Will Not Be Silenced, pages 41-42

There are a variety of ways to rewrite the past. One of the more vivid ones is the tearing down of statues and monuments dedicated not only to Confederates, but to the Founding Fathers. In some cities, government officials have had statues quietly removed in the darkness of night to appease protesters.

Another way is through the revision of historical events, turning them into something they were not. A prime example of this is the 1619 Project, which positions the arrival of slaves at Jamestown as the true moment when America was founded—and claims that slavery is what played a key role in the nation's early economic growth.

As horrible as slavery is in every way, the rightful denouncement of slavery does not excuse the wrongful denouncement of what actually took place in history. The action of bringing slaves to a nation is not what determines when it was founded. Otherwise, it would be necessary to change the founding date of the many nations that approved of slavery all over the world (and continue to do so today). It is entirely possible for us to condemn the institution of slavery without conflating it with the actual founding date of a country. In America's case, the individual colonies that predated the signing of the Declaration of Independence in 1776 had no declared identity as a nation.

What the 1619 Project fails to mention is that during the Revolutionary era, the abolition of slavery was already under way, beginning with Vermont in 1777. Five other states followed from 1780 to 1804, and more in the years prior to the US Civil War.

Also, it was the industrialized northern states—and not the south—that powered America's economic growth. As economic historians Alan L. Olmstead and Paul W. Rhode have observed, the cotton industry of the South "played no role in kick-starting the Industrial Revolution." They point out that, contrary to what the 1619 Project claims, slavery was "a national tragedy that…*inhibited* economic growth over the long run and created social and racial division that still haunt the nation."[1]

Yet another way that the secular left rewrites history is by hijacking words and changing their definitions. These new definitions are then used to advance their agenda. A classic example is the word *tolerance*. At one time, the word *tolerance* meant people of opposing viewpoints could agree to disagree, and *both* would be considered tolerant of one another. But today, merely disagreeing—even graciously—with whatever is deemed politically correct immediately gets a person branded as intolerant.

Another example of a word taken over by the secular left is *balance*. Leftists are quick to describe their political views as being balanced, which implies that anyone who disagrees with them is unbalanced. In this way, they position their policies as being fair and reasonable, and other policies as not being so.

In these ways, cultural Marxists and secularists are rewriting history and controlling the direction of political discourse so that it favors their goals.

The Destruction of Monuments

The destruction of monuments is part of a larger attempt to destroy what it means to be an American. It's an attempt to remove not just racism, but to discredit all else that was done by those who created our nation's founding documents and established the foundational principles that led to making America what it is.

We Will Not Be Silenced, page 43

While we all agree that America's history of slavery was evil, is this a legitimate reason to discard our Judeo-Christian heritage? Explain.

What do those who are trying to rebuild America according to a radical socialist agenda ignore about what capitalism has done to the country?

While we can rightly support peaceful demonstrations in support of racial equality, is destructive vengeance by mobs ever justified? Why or why not?

Does the fact America still has imperfections mean that we should destroy our entire legacy and start all over from scratch? What is a more sensible approach?

> The secularists are insisting that we turn a corner so that we lose sight of the Judeo-Christian influence of our past. And if we do choose to look back, they want us to see our religious history as a blotch, not a blessing.
>
> *We Will Not Be Silenced*, page 47

A Marxist History of the United States

One major example of historical revisionism is Howard Zinn's school textbook *A People's History of the United States*. What are some of the things this book overlooks?

America's radical critics make it sound as though the West invented slavery. What did the West actually do, and what is the state of slavery in the world today?

Why do those behind the 1619 Project fail to compare America to other countries?

When radicals use slavery to delegitimize America, what else are they attempting to delegitimize?

Denouncing Western Civilization

On page 52 of *We Will Not Be Silenced*, we read, "Racism and various other sins are rather equally distributed among all the peoples of the world; we must distinguish the positive contributions from the negative and the victories from the losses regardless of which group or race we are discussing."

In the case of Western civilization, what are some examples of positive contributions and victories we can point to?

What are some examples of positive contributions Christians and the church have made, both in the past and today?

On page 54 of *We Will Not Be Silenced*, we read, "We must listen to each other as we talk about the injustices of our shared history, acknowledging that both repentance and forgiveness are necessary. But then we must move on, or we will never be able to make progress in race relations."

This approach stands in contrast to Critical Race Theory, which divides society into groups of oppressors and the oppressed, and declares that oppressors have no voice at the table—only the oppressed. Which of the two approaches described above do you believe is more likely to produce a positive outcome, and why?

Rewriting the Constitution

As stated on pages 55-56 of *We Will Not Be Silenced*, what are some of the objectives of the secularist agenda, and for what purpose?

The Secularists' Foundation

What does *The Humanist Manifesto* advocate?

Do humanists see American exceptionalism and globalism as compatible? Explain.

To overcome the obstacles of globalism, humanists promote the concept of open borders. What two objectives do open borders achieve for humanists?

American exceptionalism is one of the terms leftists have highjacked to give it a different meaning. They have reinterpreted it to be demeaning and dismissive of other countries. But the exceptionalism refers not to an elitist attitude; rather, it speaks of how the freedoms and opportunities made available to Americans have enabled the country to prosper and enjoy a higher standard of living than most places in the world. It is these freedoms and opportunities that immigrants find so attractive, leading many to move here.

Based on this right understanding of American exceptionalism, what are some examples of it that you can think of?

Learning from History

What do we as Christians do when the history of our country is being rewritten or even deleted? And how do we respond when the cultural ground beneath us is shifting? Our calling and privilege is to represent Christ at this turbulent moment in history.

We Will Not Be Silenced, page 60

Do you agree that it is possible to learn from history without destroying it? What are one or two examples of historical teaching opportunities you can think of that would instruct us toward a better future?

What do you think America would look like if it were rebuilt on a purely secular foundation?

America, the Church, and our Future

Scripture teaches us to love our enemies (Matthew 5:44)—this includes our ideological enemies. As we respond to what is going on around us, what attitudes do you think Christ would want us to show?

Moving forward, how can the church stay rooted in the Scriptures despite the growing legal and cultural pressures to submit to the humanist agenda promoted by secularists?

What word of hope is offered on pages 64-65 of *We Will Not Be Silenced*?

In what way are you personally encouraged by this word of hope?

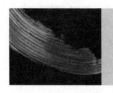

IN YOUR OWN WORDS

In 25 to 50 words, write your responses to the following questions.

What aspect of this book chapter and workbook lesson "Rewrite the Past to Control the Future" had the greatest impact on you?

How do you see this affecting the way you think and live as a Christian?

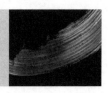
The early church father Augustine is reported to have said, "Whatever men build, men will destroy. So let's get on with building the kingdom of God." Why should building God's kingdom be of greater importance to us than attempting to reclaim today's culture?

What are some specific ways that all of us as Christians can engage in the work of doing what Christ has called us to do in the midst of a lost and dying world?

Matthew 6:19-21 says, "Do not lay up for yourselves treasures on earth, where moth and rust destroy and thieves break in and steal, but lay up for yourselves treasures in heaven, where neither moth destroys and where thieves do not break in and steal. For where your treasure is, there your heart will be also." What significance does this command from Jesus take on in the context of the historical and societal destruction happening in today's culture?

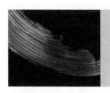

COMMITTING YOURSELF TO PRAYER

Upon completing this lesson, what five things do you desire to make a matter of prayer right now? List them here.

1.

2.

3.

4.

5.

Take a few moments now to lift these concerns up to the Lord.

> You are the light of the world. A city set on a hill cannot be hidden.
> Nor do people light a lamp and put it under a basket, but on a stand,
> and it gives light to all the house. In the same way,
> let your light shine before others, so that they may see your good works
> and give glory to your Father who is in heaven.
>
> Matthew 5:14-16

LESSON 3

Use Diversity to Divide and Destroy

Stir up discontent. Use problems. Create guilt.

Alinsky made no secret of the fact he was a committed Marxist who believed that the conflict between the oppressed and the oppressors must be continual, unending, and without a satisfactory resolution—unless, of course, there is a revolution that brings about the "equalities" of a Marxist state...So the call for change is never really about race, gender, or economic status, but revolution—and power.

There was a time when racial reconciliation was a search for common ground, seeking understanding between the races, minimizing our differences, and focusing on our similarities and shared commitments. We believed that progress was made by including the various ethnic and racial groups in businesses, educational institutions, and churches. We were committed to honoring one another.

We Will Not Be Silenced, pages 72-73

We who are Christians should be on the forefront of encouraging and living out unity in the midst of today's racial discord. Every person is a unique creation of God; the fact He made every one of us so different is a testimony to His love for diversity. And when the unifying factor is Jesus Christ, wonderful things are possible.

When we define our equality in terms of our value before God and our identity in Christ, the things that have the potential to divide us fall to the wayside. As we endeavor to love and accept one another as brothers and sisters in Christ, we will experience unity rather than division.

But secular culture has come up with its own measures of equality, insisting on a *forced* kind of equality—using whatever means necessary, including persuasion, intimidation, and shaming—to bring about equal outcomes for all people with regard to status, education, ability, income, and more. Cultural Marxists promote equal rewards for all regardless of what effort someone expends or what achievements they've accomplished. From their perspective, if one person is not successful, it is the fault of another. As we learned earlier, for cultural Marxists to advance their cause, it's necessary for them to foster the concepts of oppression and victimhood. They want to stir up strife rather than encourage people to strive for commonality.

This forced equality has been rebranded as social justice and political correctness. In this lesson, we'll take a closer look at this issue of equality—at how secular leftists use diversity as a wedge to divide people rather than encourage them to sit down, talk, listen to, and help one another.

What does it mean to be "woke"?

What are some examples of wokeness you are aware of?

The Many Faces of Equality

What are some of the ways that secular culture is striving for equality?

What does the Bible teach when it says, "Everyone to whom much was given, of him much will be required" (Luke 12:48)?

How is God's fairness seen in the parable of the man who entrusted his property to three different stewards (Matthew 25:15, 21-23, 26-27)? What will we be judged for?

When economic equality is imposed, what ends up being stamped out?

On page 78 of *We Will Not Be Silenced*, we read, "Equality of *opportunities* cannot guarantee equality in *outcomes*."

In what ways does this make sense?

The Quest for Social Justice

Biblically, what does *justice* mean?

Today, what has *justice* been separated from, and how has it become a bloated term?

What is social justice most often defined as?

What does Critical Race Theory (CRT) teach?

What kind of thinking is promoted in university courses about social justice and diversity?

What do CRT advocates tell alleged oppressors they must do?

What are those who are classified as victims urged to do?

Based on what you have learned so far, what would you say are the differences between biblical justice and social justice?

Intersectionality

What does intersectionality refer to?

What will people do when they fear being accused of bias, racism, or hatred?

CRT in the Church

On page 85 in *We Will Not Be Silenced*, we read that "in the purely secular application of CRT, redemption is viewed as separating a group from oppressors, not as the need to be freed from sin by the gospel of God's saving grace."

Given this perspective from CRT advocates, in what ways do you see CRT as disagreeing with Christianity?

CRT declares that lived experience is much more reliable than objective truth. In what ways do you see this kind of thinking problematic, and even unbiblical?

The Controversy About White Guilt

What is white guilt?

Why does black leader Shelby Steele believe that the transition from white supremacy to white guilt has not been good for the black community?

What observation did black pastor Reverend Bill Owens make about liberal social policies?

In all the debates regarding white guilt and white privilege, we would do well to remember the words of Martin Luther King Jr., who reminded us that we should not judge one another by the color of our skin but by the content of our character.

We Will Not Be Silenced, pages 89-90

The Critical Role of Families in Our National Struggles

While we should do everything we can to address racism and right the wrongs done against certain groups of people, still, there are problems within our own homes and communities that need to be dealt with as well. Ultimately, what is required to solve these "within culture" problems?

What did Theodore Dalrymple observe to be the most powerful influence that holds people down?

What did Dalrymple say is the foremost perpetrator of the underclass?

In what ways can you see strong families being a deterrent to the kinds of problems that plague those in the underclass?

How can churches be active in building strong families—both within a church itself, and in the surrounding community?

The Church in a Toxic Culture

What advantage does the church have that CRT does not have?

In Colossians, Paul lists people with racial, ethnic, cultural, and societal differences. However, rather than dividing them into categories, he sees them as united in Christ...we not only have the same Savior, but we share the same life and are stones in the same temple (1 Peter 2:5).

We Will Not Be Silenced, pages 97-98

As Christians, how can we move forward together in race relations, rather than following the culture's pattern of accusations and conflict?

On page 100 of *We Will Not Be Silenced*, we read, "Only through the cross can we show what reconciliation looks like to the world."

What does the cross offer that the world does not?

When it comes to racial reconciliation, what is the problem with leaving God out of the picture?

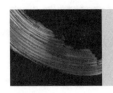

IN YOUR OWN WORDS

In 25 to 50 words, write your responses to the following questions.

What aspect of this book chapter and workbook lesson "Use Diversity to Divide and Destroy" had the greatest impact on you?

How do you see this affecting the way you think and live as a Christian?

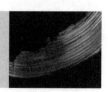

What do the following passages say about how we are to treat people?

Colossians 3:12-14—

James 2:1-13—

Nurturing strong families goes a long way to helping overcome the problems that plague the disadvantaged. Name two or three ways you and your church can be active in helping to build strong families—both within the church itself, and in the surrounding community.

The starting point toward reconciliation is listening to one another. What does it take to be a good listener?

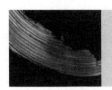

COMMITTING YOURSELF TO PRAYER

Upon completing this lesson, what five things do you desire to make a matter of prayer right now? List them here.

1.

2.

3.

4.

5.

Take a few moments now to lift these concerns up to the Lord.

Live in harmony with one another.
Do not be haughty, but associate with the lowly.
Never be wise in your own sight.
Repay no one evil for evil, but give thought
to do what is honorable in the sight of all.
If possible, so far as it depends on you,
live peaceably with all.

Romans 12:16-18

LESSON 4

Freedom of Speech for Me, but Not for Thee

Revolutions begin with a cultural moment, a pretext that will hide the real agenda to justify the revolution. You need (1) the triumph of an ideology over science, reason, and civil liberties. Then you (2) recruit people who are willing to advance the revolution of anarchy in the name of justice and equality. And finally, (3) you must silence all dissident voices. Submission to the ideology is enforced either by shaming, by laws, or simply by exclusion, such as firing opposing voices from the workplace.

We Will Not Be Silenced, page 103

Freedom of speech is what makes it possible for people to present their ideas and opinions for discussion in a public forum. This makes it possible for all options to come under consideration so that people can choose and act upon the best of those options. The free exchange of ideas is intended to give people information that enables them to make informed choices and bring about changes that are beneficial to society. When it comes to measuring the amount of freedom a country has, the top metric is freedom of speech: Are people allowed to freely share ideas without fear of reprisal?

The importance of freedom of speech is affirmed by the fact this right is enshrined in the very first amendment to the US Constitution. In basic terms, freedom of speech supports the right of a person or group to state their ideas and opinions without fear of retaliation or censorship by the government. In countries where there is no freedom of speech, ideas that are critical of government officials or policies are not permitted to be expressed.

One aspect of freedom of speech is that with it comes special responsibilities, meaning that there are certain commonsense restrictions that take into consideration the rights and reputation of others, and for national security purposes or the sake of public health. Among the limitations are prohibitions against perjury, libel, slander, incitement, classified materials, copyright violations, and the right to privacy.

Interestingly, the reason cultural Marxism is able to thrive in America is because of freedom of speech. Proponents of cultural Marxism are permitted to introduce their ideas into the public forum in an attempt to sway people toward their political viewpoints. Yet cultural Marxism's worldview states that oppressors should remain silent, and only the oppressed should be allowed to speak. It also says lived experience trumps objective truth. While cultural Marxism is quick to *claim* its right to free speech, it is even quicker to *reject* the right of others to speak, and it resorts to tactics designed to shame others into silence.

How does cancel culture work?

Do you see cancel culture as a sign of a country that is on its way to greatness, or a country in decline? Give examples, if you can.

The Value of Free Speech

How is hate speech being defined these days?

Arguments for Banning Free Speech

What was Marxist philosopher Herbert Marcuse's main argument against free speech?

Marcuse wrote that Marxists should put an end to "the liberal creed of free and equal discussion" and that they should be "militantly intolerant."[1] What evidence do you see of this kind of thinking today?

Can you give an example of how some people use free speech to argue against free speech?

Shutting Down Free Speech

What are some examples of places or forums in which only progressive thoughts are welcomed and all others are discouraged?

Why has the radical left changed from championing free speech to banning it?

Intimidation on Campus

Why do you think radical secularists believe unapproved speech should be shut down rather than debated?

According to Heather Mac Donald, what lies at the center of campus intolerance?

The Effects of Intolerance

> If the Enlightenment taught us anything, it is that freedom of speech came about through a willingness of those who held opposing viewpoints to engage in argument, discussion, and heated debate.
>
> *We Will Not Be Silenced*, page 117

What will be the end result when students—and by extension, all people—are not allowed to hear and consider alternate viewpoints?

As a Christian, in what ways are you seeing secular culture discourage the expression of a biblical worldview? Give some examples of how certain Christian teachings are criticized as being intolerant.

Arguments in Favor of Free Speech

On page 118 of *We Will Not Be Silenced*, we read, "We live in an 'offended generation.' We are being told that everyone's right to free speech should be curtailed so as not to offend anyone."

What is the danger of insisting that any speech that merely *offends* someone—no matter how politely or reasonably it is stated—should be prohibited?

On page 119 we read, "The freedom to think, interact, criticize, and discuss issues is essential for the common good...Free speech is the basis for our other freedoms."

What are some ways that freedom of speech makes other freedoms possible?

Ironically, our culture says that the radicals who censor others are being tolerant, and accuses those who adhere to traditional concepts of freedom of speech as being intolerant. What impact is this perception having on public discourse?

Why do you think Frederick Douglass declared in 1860 that free speech is "the dread of tyrants"?

The Response of the Church

There are two ways culture attempts to intimidate Christians. One is to criminalize what they say or do, and the other is to shame them. Many Christians will not be *talked* out of their faith, but they will be *mocked* out of it. Shame will cause many Christians to retreat into silence.

We Will Not Be Silenced, page 121

What are some ways we as Christians have felt pressured into silence in our communities, workplaces, or schools?

What are some examples of how Christianity is mocked publicly, including in the media?

Read Acts 4:1-20. What were Peter and John arrested for?

What threat did the religious authorities issue against Peter and John (verse 18)?

How did Peter and John respond (verses 19-20)?

On page 122 of *We Will Not Be Silenced*, we read, "The martyrs before us have shown that it is not necessary to have free speech in order to be faithful."

Give some examples from the Bible and church history that demonstrate this to be true.

When we use free speech to talk about our faith, according to the following passages, what attitudes should we exhibit?

      Colossians 4:5-6—

      1 Peter 3:15—

What is the secret of boldness?

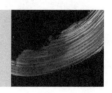

In 25 to 50 words, write your responses to the following questions.

What aspect of this book chapter and workbook lesson "Freedom of Speech for Me, but Not for Thee" had the greatest impact on you?

How do you see this affecting the way you think and live as a Christian?

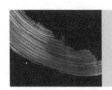

COMMITTING YOURSELF TO ACTION

On page 121 of *We Will Not Be Silenced*, we read, "Boldness comes easily when you are in the presence of those who agree with you; it is difficult when you are standing alone in the midst of people who seek your demise…Boldness is seen most clearly when you have burned the bridge that would have enabled you to retreat to safety."

What are some examples of boldness that we see in Scripture—boldness that had a high cost attached to it and sought to please God rather than people?

What does it really mean to fear God more than the flames?

Why is it so important that we not be afraid to speak the truth with love?

When you see other Christians who are bold, how does that inspire you? What would be the result if all believers were willing to be bold?

COMMITTING YOURSELF TO PRAYER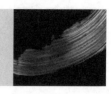

Upon completing this lesson, what five things do you desire to make a matter of prayer right now? List them here.

1.

2.

3.

4.

5.

Take a few moments now to lift these concerns up to the Lord.

Fear not, for I am with you; be not dismayed,
for I am your God; I will strengthen you, I will help you,
I will uphold you with my righteous right hand.

Isaiah 41:10

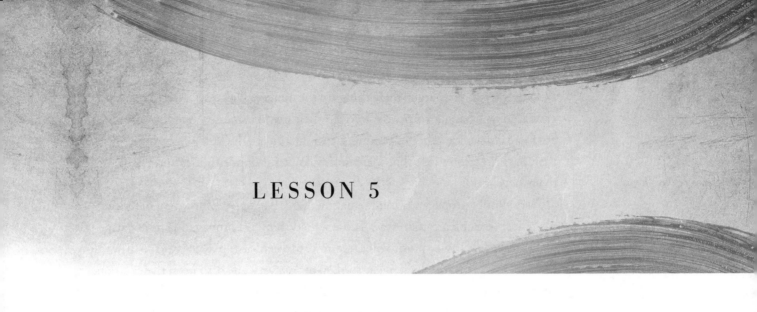

LESSON 5

Sell It as
a Noble Cause

The purpose of propaganda is to change people's perception of reality so that despite compelling counterevidence, people will not change their minds. The goal is to make people impervious to facts, scientific proof, and common sense. Of course, sometimes facts and scientific proof can be subject to interpretation. But often obvious arguments are set aside because people believe what they want to believe even in the face of mounting contrary evidence.

We Will Not Be Silenced, page 128

Propaganda is powerful. When something is said enough times, it is often treated as a truth, even when there is evidence that it's not. Through repetitious proclamation and the silencing of those who disagree, today's propaganda becomes tomorrow's "truth."

Cultural Marxists are diligent to package their ideas in ways that make them sound appealing or virtuous. For example, when they attack the capitalist economic system that has made America the prosperous nation it is, they do so under the guise of equality—they say that all wealth should be equally spread by the government, and that a person's economic reward shouldn't depend on hard work, ingenuity, and the kinds of skills they have. They argue these things in the name of fairness yet fail to mention that capitalism is what allows people to open their own businesses, be innovative and create more efficient and better products, and thus create the kind of consumer demand that, in turn, creates jobs that increase employment opportunities and enable people to get paychecks.

Very simply, propaganda is information that is biased with the intent of leading people to feel or think a certain way. Those who depend on propaganda to persuade people to accept their viewpoint will often resort to censorship as they do so. They don't want their ideas to be challenged, so they make every effort to keep their opponents silent. This is consistent with how cultural Marxists operate today—if you don't agree with what they say about race, then you are branded as racist. They position their view as the correct one and slander everyone else's view as being wrong.

The most effective defense against propaganda is an abundance of information, which is why those who spread propaganda also work so hard to control the flow of information. This is what we see happen in George Orwell's novel *1984*—the Ministry of Truth and Thought Police worked to brainwash people to think in certain ways. Similarly, today's cultural Marxists have appointed themselves as the judges of what is considered true and acceptable—and what isn't.

During World War II, what ironic slogan appeared on the entry gates of several of Adolf Hitler's concentration camps?

When radicals hear a viewpoint they don't like, they say, "I don't like the message, so I will just destroy the messenger." Give two or three examples of how you've seen this happen.

In the garden of Eden, the serpent enticed Adam and Eve with fruit that looked good so he could persuade them to take something bad. What are some ways you see this kind of deception happening today?

How Propaganda Works

What are the different forms that propaganda takes?

Appealing to a Higher Goal

Why is so much of advertising based not so much on *need*, but on *desire*?

On page 131 of *We Will Not Be Silenced*, we read, "Even evil, if packaged correctly, can appear to be good, and good can be packaged as evil."

What are some examples of this in today's culture?

How may we find ourselves attempting to use propaganda to package evil as good? (For example, what are some ways that we justify giving in to temptation?)

Using Slogans to Mask Evil

Write down a couple examples of deceptive slogans mentioned in *We Will Not Be Silenced*.

What are a couple more examples you've seen used by people or in the media?

Hitler, Propaganda, and the Power of Hate

Summarize how Hitler used propaganda to gradually move the German people toward hatred of the Jewish people.

On page 135 of *We Will Not Be Silenced*, we read, "If hate did not keep people in line, fear would."

What are some reasons that we as Christians find ourselves afraid to push back against deception or propaganda?

Creating a Cultural Stream

> A population in panic mode is easily led. Or rather, misled.
>
> *We Will Not Be Silenced*, page 139

During the COVID-19 crisis, what were some ways people were willing to change their behavior or do things they normally wouldn't do? (You can give examples either from the book or from your personal experience.)

What are some other ways we see fear being used today to motivate people to change their behavior?

The Power of Collective Demonization

What is collective demonization?

How do we see collective demonization being used in our culture?

In what ways do we see people being vilified through social media?

Propaganda and the Sexual Revolution

Summarize the strategy that gay activists used to change people's attitudes about homosexuality.

What is one of the oldest schemes of propaganda? And why is this so effective?

Sell It as a Civil Right

What was the "high moral ground" that activists used to portray the normalization of homosexual relationships as a noble cause?

What important ally do homosexuals and transgenders have on their side, and how does this ally help them?

Sell It as Love and Compassion

On page 145 of *We Will Not Be Silenced*, we read, "People often do not perceive reality as it is but how they want it to be."

Why do you think people do this?

What are some ways we see the banner of love being used to normalize things that are unbiblical?

Is it possible for love to be sinful? Explain.

What instruction did Jesus give in John 14:15 for showing our love for Him?

On page 146 of *We Will Not Be Silenced*, we read, "Love and sympathy can be misused to override our better judgment."

What are some ways you've seen this happen?

Gaslighting in Our Modern Culture

What is gaslighting?

What is the purpose of gaslighting?

> We are to be good citizens carried along by a herd mentality; we are expected to accept a reality that is bent to suit an ideology.
>
> *We Will Not Be Silenced,* page 148

Using Language to Destroy Gender

How are pronouns being manipulated to fit with the transgender cultural stream?

Can you think of other ways language is being manipulated to favor the latest trends for what is considered culturally acceptable or unacceptable?

Changing Language to Lower the Crime Rate

From page 150 of *We Will Not Be Silenced*, cite two or three examples of how language is being used to minimize crime.

For what reason is this being done?

Why does the radical left's "sanitizing" of language make honest dialogue difficult?

The Response of the Church

What price might we have to pay for taking a stand against the destructive cultural currents prevailing in society today?

What are some examples of unbiblical perspectives that Christians are being persuaded to accept in today's culture?

Read 2 Corinthians 4:2. In what manner should we as Christians conduct ourselves when it comes to handling God's Word?

Take time to figure out some of the differences that characterize propagandists and truth-tellers. The first one is done for you.

Propagandists	Truth-Tellers
1. Manipulate the facts	Do not alter the facts
2.	
3.	
4.	
5.	

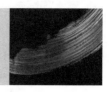

In 25 to 50 words, write your responses to the following questions.

What aspect of this book chapter and workbook lesson "Sell It as a Noble Cause" had the greatest impact on you?

How do you see this affecting the way you think and live as a Christian?

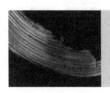

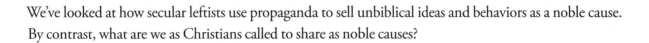

COMMITTING YOURSELF TO ACTION

We've looked at how secular leftists use propaganda to sell unbiblical ideas and behaviors as a noble cause. By contrast, what are we as Christians called to share as noble causes?

Why is integrity in your personal life and your ministry so important in a world so full of deception?

What are three or four ways you can graciously advance the truth to people you know who are caught in culture's stream? Come up with specific ideas for speaking the truth or acting on it. Then commit these ideas to prayer and ask the Lord to open doors for you.

COMMITTING YOURSELF TO PRAYER

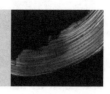

Upon completing this lesson, what five things do you desire to make a matter of prayer right now? List them here.

1.

2.

3.

4.

5.

Take a few moments now to lift these concerns up to the Lord.

> Praying always…that I may open my mouth boldly
> to make known the mystery of the gospel,
> for which I am an ambassador in chains;
> that in it I may speak boldly, as I ought to speak.
>
> Ephesians 6:18-19

LESSON 6

Sexualize the Children

Perhaps nowhere do we see the work of Satan in America as clearly as we do in the sexualization of children—destroying their identity, confusing their gender, and creating unresolved guilt and self-hatred. Jesus warned, "Whoever receives one such child in my name receives me, but whoever causes one of these little ones who believe in me to sin, it would be better for him to have a great millstone fastened around his neck and to be drowned in the depth of the sea" (Matthew 18:5-6).

We Will Not Be Silenced, page 156

We have all heard the expression that children are like soft clay—they are easily shaped by whatever influences are molding them. We also know that, in time, clay hardens—which is why it's so essential for parents and other family members to expose children to biblical ways of thinking as early and often as possible.

In today's hyper-technological world, raising children has become more challenging than ever. With smartphones, the internet, and social media, a child is exposed to many ideas contrary to the instruction they receive from their parents and at church. Public schools feed an unending stream of secular and progressive thinking to youth who haven't yet been trained to critically evaluate what they are reading and hearing.

And because parents are left in the dark as to how their children are being influenced, they frequently are unaware of the need to provide a counterresponse that will help keep their children out of harm's way. All this requires parents and families to be as proactive as possible about instructing their children so that they can discern right from wrong, good from bad.

The corrupting of children is no superficial matter. They are being challenged to the very core of their being, especially with regard to their sexual identity. They are being sold a way of thinking that destroys all the biblical and traditional principles about moral decency and normal sexuality. That which God designed to be private and sacred is being made public and defiled.

One key reason God placed strict boundaries around all matters having to do with sex is that a right view of sexuality is one of the most fundamental elements of holy and pure living. A person who has broken away from God's design for sexuality isn't going to be concerned about maintaining right thinking or behavior in other areas of their life. That is why sexual sin is so dangerous, and why God takes it so seriously.

For us to protect our young ones, we need to understand what is happening and to provide consistent biblical guidance that equips our children to make right choices in response to all the varied forms of deviant thinking they are exposed to.

The Corrupting Influence of Our Public Schools

What observation did Peter Hitchens make about children in his book *The Rage Against God*?

What is cultural Marxism's goal when it comes to education?

Who determines what is taught in public schools today?

What kinds of ideas about sexuality are promoted in the *Comprehensive Sexuality Education* curriculum?

What did researchers discover about the influence of early sexual education, as reported in "The Effect of Early Sexual Activity on Mental Health"?

What deceptive language is used to sell the new sexual curriculum?

Christian Colleges Submit to LGBTQ Values

With regard to LGBTQ policies, what kind of pressure are Christian colleges and seminaries under?

This same pressure is being applied to Christian ministries, businesses, and churches. What are the only two options available, and in your opinion, what will be the results of following those options?

The Larger Culture Goes Woke

The sexual revolution continues to accelerate, taking everything in its wake. Given its disdain for biology, science, and decency, it intends to destroy the very concept of masculinity and femininity in a child's earliest ages. Social justice requires it.

We Will Not Be Silenced, page 162

What are some of the ways we see transgenderism being sold as normal and acceptable?

On page 164 of *We Will Not Be Silenced*, we read, "Progress in the wrong direction is not something to celebrate—especially when it goes against the natural order of creation or even the established facts of science."

What kind of fallout do you see in our society as a result of this sexual "progress" in the wrong direction?

In contrast, what are the benefits that result when we live according to a biblical worldview, especially with regard to sexual values?

What Next?

On page 165 of *We Will Not Be Silenced*, we read, "Without God, there is no reason for anyone to say no to the most perverse, previously unimaginable sexual relationships."

Why does it make sense that once God is pushed out of the way, everything will go downhill?

What accusations are made against Christians who attempt to help individuals who want to leave the homosexual or transgender lifestyle? Why do you think secular culture is so adamantly against this kind of help?

The Demonic Nature of What's Happening in the Transgender Phenomenon

When it comes to the transgender movement, what is happening with parental rights?

Where Is the Church?

What do you think are the best ways for Christian parents to respond to a child who says he or she is gay or transgender?

We must return to the creation account to remind ourselves that God created only two genders: male and female. Without a belief in God as Creator, there is little hope of making sense of our lives and the roles we are intended to have in marriage, the family, and of course, sexuality.

We Will Not Be Silenced, page 171

On page 172 of *We Will Not Be Silenced*, we read, "Only when we recognize the human heart's propensity to deception are we able to help others see their problems from a divine perspective. Remember, those who walk in darkness do not see things as they are, but rather, see things the way they want them to be."

Why do you think it is important to help deceived people see their problems from a divine perspective?

For the deceived person who is genuinely looking for help, what Scripture passages can you share that would offer hope?

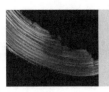

IN YOUR OWN WORDS

In 25 to 50 words, write your responses to the following questions.

What aspect of this book chapter and workbook lesson "Sexualize the Children" had the greatest impact on you?

How do you see this affecting the way you think and live as a Christian?

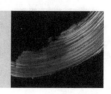
What are some constructive ways to keep children from becoming addicted to their smartphone and computers, and to protect them from the negative effects of social media?

How do we as parents, family members, or church members contribute to the seductive values of our culture by what we watch, how we relate to others, and the value we place on personal purity?

Think of parents or a family with a child who has been negatively influenced or harmed by culture. What are one or two ways you can offer meaningful help—either to the child or the parents?

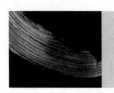

COMMITTING YOURSELF TO PRAYER

Upon completing this lesson, what five things do you desire to make a matter of prayer right now? List them here.

1.

2.

3.

4.

5.

Take a few moments now to lift these concerns up to the Lord.

> See to it that no one takes you captive by philosophy and empty deceit,
> according to human tradition, according to the elemental spirits of the world,
> and not according to Christ.
>
> Colossians 2:8

Capitalism Is the Disease; Socialism Is the Cure

What is socialism? In a nutshell, it is the supremacy of the state over the individual. Or if you want a one-word definition, it's *statism*. It's when the government takes ownership of the means of production and promises to redistribute wealth in what is claimed to be a fair-minded way. On the surface, this seems like an attractive solution to poverty and fiscal insecurity.

We Will Not Be Silenced, page 178

One feature of socialism that makes it so attractive is the claim that in a socialist world, no one will be left behind. Everyone will be on an even playing field because everyone is assured of income equality.

Socialism's main criticism of capitalism is that it is oppressive—that wealthy people exploit the poor, who will remain poor because the rich are greedy and use their power to perpetuate a continuing state of class exploitation. The solution? The government must confiscate all private property and redistribute it to achieve justice and equality.

While capitalism can be abused, a comparison of capitalistic and socialistic economies worldwide reveals that the standard of living is consistently higher in capitalistic countries. That's because only in a capitalistic economy can businesses generate the wealth that is necessary to bring more opportunities—that is, jobs—to a greater number of people. It is this abundance of opportunities and jobs that has made the United States so attractive to people all over the world who want to better their lot in life.

What socialists don't like to say is that for their system to work, the government must have control of everything—including people's rights. Because the government has become the self-appointed arbiter who decides how to "spread the wealth," among other things, it is the government that decides what people can and cannot do. The same state that decides how money is going to be distributed will also decide how people's rights are distributed. The very system that claims to empower the people actually removes power from them. It's no mere coincidence that, on the freedom scale, socialist countries are far more restrictive than nonsocialist ones, and they have governments that are more authoritarian.

No matter how many promises socialism offers, it only hurts people and is destined to fail, for reasons we'll see in this lesson.

Yes, Marx Does, in Fact, Rule from the Grave

What concerned Marx about England's industrial revolution?

What three beliefs did Marx base his views on?

Why did Marx hate Christianity?

What was Marx's view of mothers and the family?

What did Marx say about laws?

What happens when a government says that it is the state that creates rights, and not God?

Why does Marxism look so attractive to people who live in Latin America and Russia?

What are some of the things capitalism is blamed for?

Cultural Marxism or Democratic Socialism

What does democratic socialism—also known as cultural Marxism—promise to do?

Based on what we've learned so far about socialism, why does it make sense that democratic socialism eventually leads to a form of democratic totalitarianism?

The Importance of Climate Change

Briefly, what are the two reasons radical secularists are so adamant about climate change?

> As Christians, we most assuredly should be good stewards of the environment. God gave us the world of nature and animals not to exploit, but to use responsibly. We will give an account for our stewardship. Reducing the use of plastics, properly disposing of waste, and dozens of other environmentally conscientious actions should be on our agenda. Yet we should also distinguish the Creator from the creature.
>
> *We Will Not Be Silenced*, page 186

A Case Study of Democratic Socialism

Ultimately, why is it that socialism cannot keep its promises for very long?

Democratic socialists point to Sweden as a success story, citing the country as evidence that their kind of socialism works. But what has actually happened in Sweden?

What happened in Venezuela after the government took control of the means of production?

Marvin Olasky is quoted as saying, "Socialism…crushes ambition in pursuit of a uniform, unfulfilling and arbitrary definition of 'equality.' And it does all of this in the name of 'the greater good.'" What additional thoughts does this observation give you about socialism's inability to deliver on its promises?

COVID-19 Bailouts and the Push for Socialism

Stepping Toward Socialism

During the COVID-19 crisis, in what ways did governing authorities exercise greater than usual power, and why do you think these government actions serve as indicators we are moving more toward socialism?

The Making of Fiat Money

What is fiat money, and does it have any real value?

Does the Bible Teach Socialism?

What are at least a couple evidences that socialism is not found in the Bible?

What does "the Protestant work ethic" teach?

In what ways do the following passages affirm the concept of private ownership rather than government?

Exodus 20:17—

Leviticus 25:10—

Deuteronomy 19:14—

Deuteronomy 22:1-4—

Economic Theory and Human Nature

What is the only way that capitalism works?

Under capitalism, why is power in the hands of the consumer?

Where does power lie in socialism, and what is the result?

Why do socialists always talk about spreading wealth but not about creating it?

> Which economic system is more compassionate? The one that, of necessity, has to meet the needs of its customers? Or the one that can operate without any thought for benefitting people?
>
> *We Will Not Be Silenced*, page 198

Greed and Corruption

What is the fatal flaw of socialism?

Why does socialism give more opportunity for greed and corruption than capitalism?

On page 202 of *We Will Not Be Silenced*, we read, "The more the state owns, the more it controls its citizens. The more it controls its citizens, the more it limits their freedoms."

What two or three examples can you think of that confirm these principles?

The Response of the Church

What has capitalism given to Christians in the West, and what has been the result?

In what way does money make the same promises God does? Can money keep those promises? Why or why not?

What did Jesus teach in Luke 16:9 about money?

When Francis Schaeffer urged us to have "capitalism with compassion," what was he talking about?

Read Luke 12:48. How does this affect your thoughts about money?

Our love and sacrifice should be an attractive alternative to the false hopes of utopian dreams. And even where Karl Marx still rules, the church is called to be the church.

To whom much is given, much is required.

We Will Not Be Silenced, page 206

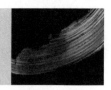

In 25 to 50 words, write your responses to the following questions.

What aspect of this book chapter and workbook lesson "Capitalism Is the Disease; Socialism Is the Cure" had the greatest impact on you?

How do you see this affecting the way you think and live as a Christian?

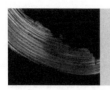

COMMITTING YOURSELF TO ACTION

While Scripture affirms the concept of privately owned property (as evidenced by the commands not to covet or steal things that belong to someone else), at the same time, the Bible urges us to give in proportion to how God has blessed us (Deuteronomy 16:10, 17). Why do you think giving is so important? As you answer, think in these terms:

Why giving is so important to God—

Why giving is so important for me—

Why giving is so important for those who benefit from my gifts—

One of the main criticisms against capitalism is that it leads to greed. What can we do as Christians to protect ourselves from succumbing to greed, and thus exhibit a right attitude toward money before the watchful eyes of others?

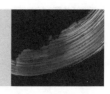

Upon completing this lesson, what five things do you desire to make a matter of prayer right now? List them here.

1.

2.

3.

4.

5.

Take a few moments now to lift these concerns up to the Lord.

> An overseer, as God's steward, must be above reproach.
> He must not be…greedy for gain.
>
> Titus 1:7

LESSON 8

Join with Radical Islam to Destroy America

Why would two ideologies—one radically secular and one radically and oppressively religious—find common ground in the United States? And why are these two groups joining hands in their attacks on basic Judeo-Christian values? Radical Islamists and racial secularists are fighting side by side, brought together by a common enemy.

We Will Not Be Silenced, page 207

W hile the majority of Muslims who live in Western society are peaceful citizens who benefit from the West's freedoms and opportunities, there is a disproportionally vocal minority of radical Islamists who are determined to impose their extremist views and convictions on all people. As the cofounder of CAIR (Council of American-Islamic Relations) said, "Islam isn't in America to be equal to any other faith, but to become dominant. The Koran should be the highest authority in America, and Islam the only accepted religion on earth."[1]

While these outspoken Islamists are pursing what they believe to be a religious ideal, today's secular leftists are endeavoring to bring about their own kind of utopia. In many areas, there are vivid differences between the two groups. Radical Islamists are very strongly opposed to the secular left's views on issues relating to religion, laws, equality, women, gender, and sexuality. The differences are so striking that it's hard to understand why the two work together to undermine America as they do.

Yet as the saying goes, "The enemy of my enemy is my friend." Both radical Islamists and the secular left view Christians, their values, and capitalism as threats that must be destroyed. In this way, they share a common goal: to overturn America's Judeo-Christian heritage and influence. To both, America needs to be de-Christianized before their utopias can be realized.

What makes this multifront battle difficult to defend against is that it's being fought through deception and manipulation. In earlier lessons, we've already seen how information is being controlled and words are being hijacked to push agendas that are hostile to America and Christianity. In this lesson, we'll learn more about the deceptive tactics at work in this battle.

Why should we not be surprised that the number of terror attacks in America have diminished? And what is "stealth jihad"?

The Opportunity of 9/11

What narrative did both Islamists and radical leftists promote after 9/11?

What have both factions blamed America for?

What naïve notion do cultural Marxists hold to?

On page 213 of *We Will Not Be Silenced*, we read that "the left believes that if capitalism were uprooted and a socialist state were to emerge, radical Islam would no longer have to be radical."

Why is this flawed thinking on the part of the left?

The Unity of Mosque and State

We all know how the radical left is adamant about the separation of church and state. By contrast, what are some examples of how there is no separation of mosque and state?

How are the tax dollars of American citizens being used to benefit Islam?

Based on what you see happening today, comparatively speaking, how is Christianity being treated differently than Islam in the public square?

If those on the left were genuinely concerned about the integrity of the First Amendement (as they interpret it), the same alleged wall that separates church and state would also separate mosque and state.

We Will Not Be Silenced, page 216

Why are leftists silent about Islam's treatment of women and homosexuals?

The Muslim Doctrine of Immigration

Why is immigration such a crucial part of Islam's goal of Islamizing America?

What is the first major point of the Muslim Brotherhood's plan for America?

The Deception of Political Correctness

On page 218, we read that "the reality is that everyone discriminates." What are some common, everyday ways we discriminate?

What has been the result of political correctness divorced from common sense?

Why have our national security agencies become paralyzed in their ability to provide their protective services?

How is the term *Islamophobia* being used—and abused?

The Response of the Church

How should we as Christians view Muslims, and why?

While on the surface the concept of interfaith dialogue may seem noble, what kind of flawed thinking is it based on?

What is the best means of introducing Muslims to the gospel?

Many of us pray for countries that are closed to the gospel and help support missionaries sent to Muslim nations. What if part of God's answer to our prayers for the Muslim world is to bring Muslims to America so they can be introduced to genuine Christians and not the caricatures promoted in their home countries?

We Will Not Be Silenced, page 222

Why is it necessary for our witness to be coupled with discernment?

On page 223 of *We Will Not Be Silenced*, we read that Christians should be taught "to be ready to die as martyrs for the faith!"

Why does it make sense that we as Christians should be prepared for—and not be afraid of—the possibility of martyrdom?

Though we will probably not be faced with martyrdom, why is it essential that we possess courage armed with truth?

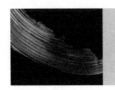

IN YOUR OWN WORDS

In 25 to 50 words, write your responses to the following questions.

What aspect of this book chapter and workbook lesson "Join with Radical Islam to Destroy America" had the greatest impact on you?

How do you see this affecting the way you think and live as a Christian?

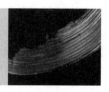

COMMITTING YOURSELF TO ACTION

The best way we as Christians can minister to Muslims is *not* to see them as enemies, but to develop genuine, caring friendships with them—even if they're not open to hearing about Jesus and the gospel. The key is this: When an opportunity does arise to share your faith, are you ready to do so?

As Christians, we should always be ready to share our faith with any unbeliever. Below are some key passages that present the path to salvation. Read them, then write, in your own words, what you need to share so that an unbeliever can know how to receive Christ as Savior.

Romans 3:23—

Romans 6:33—

Romans 5:8—

Romans 10:9-10—

Romans 10:13—

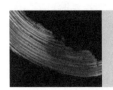

COMMITTING YOURSELF TO PRAYER

Upon completing this lesson, what five things do you desire to make a matter of prayer right now? List them here.

1.

2.

3.

4.

5.

Take a few moments now to lift these concerns up to the Lord.

> We use God's mighty weapons, not worldly weapons,
> to knock down the strongholds of human reasoning
> and to destroy false arguments.
>
> 2 Corinthians 10:4 (NLT)

Vilify! Vilify! Vilify!

The radical secularists are not satisfied with "live and let live." Rather, they demand that we totally capitulate to their agenda. And they have discovered that vilifying those who disagree with them gets more results than reason and civility.

We Will Not Be Silenced, page 225

Radical secularists aren't interested in rational discussion and arriving at a conclusion based on careful reasoning and consensus. When it comes to the cultural issues at the forefront of society, they have already reached their verdicts, and in doing so, they have followed Marxist ways of thinking: Those whom they consider to be the oppressed and victims are to be given a voice, and those whom they allege are the oppressors and privileged should be silenced. In siding with those who, from *their* perspective, are victims, they deem themselves to be tolerant and virtuous.

Yet this "tolerance" is viciously intolerant of anyone who disagrees with them. Anyone who dares to question what they say about justice, equality, race, gender, freedom of speech, the traditional family, and more is either racist or bigoted, period. Their main weapons for discourse are slander and intimidation.

This sets up what is an essentially impossible situation to navigate. When radical secularists say, for example, "All whites are racist with no exceptions, and it is impossible for people of color to be racist," they have framed the discussion in such stark absolutes that no room is allowed for any kind of discourse whatsoever, no matter how much sense it makes and how well it fits the true facts of the situation. What a victim merely perceives or claims to be true, even when it clearly isn't, is said to be more valid and true than actual facts. Dialogue is not welcome.

On this basis, the battle lines have been marked by the secular left, with every deliberate intention of stirring division rather than seeking unity. Instead of pursuing solutions that extol good character qualities among *all* people and punishing bad character qualities among *all* people, cultural Marxists believe it is necessary to destroy one class of people in order to raise up another. In the end, they are actually seeking equality only for some rather than for all, and they are exhibiting tolerance only for some rather than all.

Having drawn the battle lines in this fashion, they carry out their attacks, using criticism, intimidation, and threats in place of civility, reason, and dialogue.

What did activist Saul Alinsky mean by the concept of polarizing the target?

What are some examples you see of this happening today?

Public Shaming

Proposition 8

What did Proposition 8 define marriage as?

In what ways were supporters of Proposition 8 shamed?

What chilling effect do you think these kinds of shaming tactics can have on people?

Private Schools

What kind of pressure is being placed on private schools today?

In what ways do you see this pressure creating no-win situations for the private schools and the parents who send their kids to these schools?

Shame! Shame! Shame!

Denunciation in the Public Square

What made the protests described in pages 229-230 of *We Will Not Be Silenced* so surprising?

Vilification on Campus

What does it mean to be "doxed"?

How do activists justify their violence?

Hitler's Brownshirts and Antifa's Black Masks

What parallel did a *Jerusalem Post* op-ed piece make between the aftermath of the rioting in America during the summer of 2020 and *Kristallnacht*?

What does Antifa promote itself as being, and how do the followers of this political movement seek to accomplish their objective?

What do radicals know will happen when police forces are defunded?

What will be the natural result of vilifying the police?

What has made police forces reluctant to do crime prevention?

The Search for Allies

On page 236 of *We Will Not Be Silenced*, we read, "Certainly we should reach out with love and compassion to those who struggle with same-sex attraction, but we should also abide by what Scripture says. While we are to be kind and gracious, we are not called to become allies by bowing the knee to cultural pressure."

What are some ways we as Christians can show love and compassion without bowing to cultural pressure?

What do you think happens to our Christian witness when we do bow to cultural pressure?

The Roots of Injustice

What did David Horowitz, based on his experience, determine to be the source of injustice? And what does he say injustice is the result of?

What observation does Horowitz make about the politically correct?

Do Horowitz's observations line up with what Scripture says about humanity? Explain.

What is the only way human nature can be changed?

Coming Soon to a Church Near You

Read again the story about the church in Missouri that was vilified for teaching that God created only two genders. What does this example tell us about the challenge that churches will face in the future?

On page 241 of *We Will Not Be Silenced* we read, "Within our churches are many people who struggle with their sexual identities who are not a part of the militant minority who demonize those who disagree with them. There are many who suffer silently, not intending to impose their ideology on others, but seeking hope and healing. We need to be there for them."

What good results become possible when we as Christians are willing to continue ministering to those who struggle in spite of the backlash that might come our way?

The Response of the Church

We must remain strong, restrained, and compassionate. We should not only pray for protection from those who attack us, but also pray that we might not be afraid. When attacked, the people in the early church did not ask God to remove the persecution. Rather, they prayed that they would face it fearlessly: "Lord, look upon their threats and grant to your servants to continue to speak your word with all boldness" (Acts 4:29).

We Will Not Be Silenced, pages 241-242

With the above words in mind, ponder the following questions and write your answers:

When we as Christians become fearful of speaking the truth, what do we lose?

When we are willing to speak in the face of threats, what do we gain?

How should we view those who oppose us?

What encouragement does Matthew 5:11-12 offer to us when we are falsely accused?

Give examples, from the Bible and church history, of times when Christians were falsely accused and how they responded.

We don't have to shout louder than others when we stand our ground. We just need to know that we are being faithful to our Commander and King.

We Will Not Be Silenced, page 243

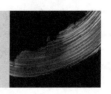

In 25 to 50 words, write your responses to the following questions.

What aspect of this book chapter and workbook lesson "Vilify! Vilify! Vilify!" had the greatest impact on you?

How do you see this affecting the way you think and live as a Christian?

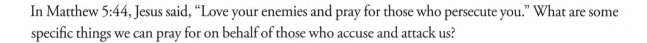

COMMITTING YOURSELF TO ACTION

In Matthew 5:44, Jesus said, "Love your enemies and pray for those who persecute you." What are some specific things we can pray for on behalf of those who accuse and attack us?

What does it mean to be a welcoming church to those who disagree with us, and at the same time, not affirm their views? How does this look in practice?

Social media has contributed significantly to this age of outrage. What guidelines should Christians follow when they post their views and responses on social media?

COMMITTING YOURSELF TO PRAYER

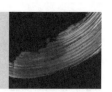

Upon completing this lesson, what five things do you desire to make a matter of prayer right now? List them here.

1.

2.

3.

4.

5.

Take a few moments now to lift these concerns up to the Lord.

> If anyone suffers as a Christian, let him not be ashamed,
> but let him glorify God in that name…
> let those who suffer according to the will of God
> entrust their souls to a faithful Creator while doing good.
>
> 1 Peter 4:16, 19

LESSON 10

Wake Up!
Strengthen What Remains!

The above words were spoken by Jesus to a church He loved.

How much of the culture should we embrace in order to redeem it? That's a question that has been endlessly discussed throughout the history of the church. There are some aspects of the culture we can embrace, but there is much that must be opposed. Our ability to discern what we can and cannot embrace is critical to the continuation of our witness as a church.

We Will Not Be Silenced, page 245

As we go about our daily lives, it is easy for us to become so preoccupied by our routines and obligations that we forget to live with an eternal perspective. We are very aware that we're citizens of earth, and we think little about the fact we are also citizens of heaven.

As ambassadors of Christ, we have a purpose that is bigger than any earthly goal or responsibility we might have. Jesus prayed to the Father, "As you sent me into the world, so I have sent them into the world" (John 17:18). The Father sent Christ to bring the good news, and He, in turn, has sent us to spread it to others.

The apostle Peter wrote, "You are a chosen race, a royal priesthood, a holy nation, a people for his own possession, *that you may proclaim the excellencies* of him who called you out of darkness into his marvelous light" (1 Peter 2:9). You are here to proclaim Him!

When it comes to representing Christ, our conduct is important. First Peter 2:12 admonishes, "Keep your conduct among the Gentiles honorable, so that when they speak against you as evildoers, they may see your good deeds and glorify God on the day of visitation." In Philippians 2:15 we're urged to "be blameless and innocent, children of God without blemish in the midst of a crooked and twisted generation, among whom you shine as lights in the world." As we read verses like these, we are reminded of the greater purpose God has called us to—a purpose we are to live out every single day: to live distinctively as Christians so that people may see God in us.

Many believers today are doing the opposite—they attempt to blend in with unbelievers, thinking that somehow, doing so gains favor among them. They seek to fit in with the world in the hopes of reaching the world. In doing this, however, they lose their distinctiveness and neglect their high calling as Christians. They render themselves ineffective for God's use.

The apostle Paul wrote in 2 Timothy 2:4, "No soldier gets entangled in civilian pursuits, since his aim is to please the one who enlisted him." God has enlisted you for a task: to shine His light into a dark world. For this reason, "let us lay aside every weight, and the sin which so easily ensnares us, and let us run with endurance the race that is set before us, looking unto Jesus, the author and finisher of our faith" (Hebrews 12:1-2).

What are some of the plusses and minuses you see in the church today? In what areas are we seeing Christians compromise, and in what areas are we seeing them be strong?

Compromise

1.

2.

3.

4.

5.

Strong

1.

2.

3.

4.

5.

What had the people at the church in Sardis done that led Jesus to describe them as dead?

According to Revelation 13:4, was there still any hope for this church?

What criticisms have progressive Christians made against historic Christianity?

On page 247 of *We Will Not Be Silenced*, we read, "As contemporary culture grows more intolerant of historic Christianity, the church is lured into accommodation and ends up being absorbed by the world. The lamp flickers, and then goes out."

Do you agree with this assessment? Why or why not?

Hearing the Voice of Jesus Today

"Be resolved to be gospel-driven in your life and witness."

What mandate did Jesus give in Mark 16:15?

What observation did Jesus make in Matthew 9:37?

What are many of today's younger Christians choosing to devote themselves to?

Are we really being bigoted and judgmental when we say Jesus is the only way to God and heaven? Explain.

If compassion motivates us to help alleviate the suffering in this present world, how much more should compassion motivate us to share the good news to alleviate their suffering in the world to come.

We Will Not Be Silenced, page 250

"Be resolved that you will not bow to the culture's sexual revolution."

According to John 17:17, what is it that sanctifies us?

What do you think happens, then, when we diminish the place truth has in our lives?

What does Paul admonish us to do in 1 Thessalonians 4:1-2?

What does Paul then say is God's will for us in verses 3-4?

What does verse 7 say God has called us to, and according to verse 8, who do we disregard when we choose to live impurely?

On page 251 of *We Will Not Be Silenced,* we read that in progressive Christianity, "doctrine is reinterpreted or even rejected to justify what the heart really wants."

What are some ways we see Christians diminishing or setting aside biblical truth in order to accommodate worldly views about sexual issues?

When Christians fail to identify sexual sin for what it really is, what do you think are the consequences for the church? For unbelievers?

How did the apostle Paul preface his teachings about sexuality in 1 Corinthians 6:9 and Galatians 6:7?

Why do you think it is so easy for Christians to allow themselves to become deluded by matters relating to sexual brokenness or impurity?

How did Jesus bring emotional and spiritual healing to the sexually broken? That is, what did He *not* do, and what did He do?

Someone has well said, "Truth without humility is judgmentalism; humility without truth is cowardice." May we be characterized by both humility and truth.

We Will Not Be Silenced, page 257

"Be resolved to love Me passionately and suffer well for My name."

In what way do we confirm our love for Christ, according to John 14:15?

Here we read that much of evangelical Christianity is "weak because our love for Christ is weak; our love of worldly values is greater than our love for Christ." Why does it make sense that the measure of our love for Christ will determine the measure of our strength or weakness as Christians?

Read 1 John 2:15-17. What stands out to you most about this warning?

A big part of the world's influence on our lives comes through our televisions, smart-phones, and computers. What are some lines we can draw to protect ourselves from a world that crashes into our lives through technology?

A Final Word from Jesus to Us

The church at Sardis had a reputation for being alive, but when Jesus applied the stethoscope, He could not find a heartbeat. What do you think defines the difference between a Christianity that merely goes through the motions, and a faith that is truly alive?

Read John 15:18 and 16:33. What comfort can we receive from these passages?

Let us resolve as a church that we will not bow to intimidation...As we persevere, let us always be ready to graciously give a defense to anyone who asks the reason for the hope within us (see 1 Peter 3:15).

We Will Not Be Silenced, page 262

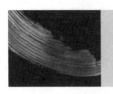

IN YOUR OWN WORDS

In 25 to 50 words, write your responses to the following questions.

What aspect of this book chapter and workbook lesson "Wake Up! Strengthen What Remains!" had the greatest impact on you?

How do you see this affecting the way you think and live as a Christian?

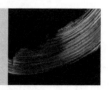

Read the entire letter that Jesus wrote to the church in Sardis (Revelation 3:1-6). What are some specific ways we can make sure we do not succumb to the same temptations that afflicted the church in Sardis?

What do you think Jesus would say if He were to write a letter to the American church? In your answer, include both compromises and strengths.

In Psalm 139:23-24, King David said, "Search me, O God, and know my heart! Try me and know my thoughts! And see if there be any grievous way in me." Why is this a good prayer for us to lift up daily? Commit yourself to doing so.

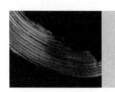

COMMITTING YOURSELF TO PRAYER

Upon completing this lesson, what five things do you desire to make a matter of prayer right now? List them here.

1.

2.

3.

4.

5.

Take a few moments now to lift these concerns up to the Lord.

This is the love of God, that we keep his commandments.
And his commandments are not burdensome.
For everyone who has been born of God overcomes the world.
And this is the victory that has overcome the world—our faith.

1 John 5:3-4

PART 2

How Should We View Our Place in Today's Culture?

How Should We View Our Place in Today's Culture?[1]

Morally speaking, Western culture is in a freefall. All of us are concerned about the rampant immorality around us. We agree that something needs to be done about the many evils that tear at the very fabric of our families and culture.

The question, of course, is this: What should be done? After all, it is difficult—if not impossible—for us to persuade non-Christians to abide by biblical moral standards. Unbelievers resent us and accuse us of "imposing our morality" on culture. They see the Bible's restrictions as the enemy of their freedom, which they believe is their inherent "right."

Every time we dare to voice biblical truth or present the Christian worldview, the pushback is powerful. We are unfairly characterized as intolerant and unloving. This, of course, gives them the appearance of being on the high ground, of being tolerant and inclusive, when in reality, their attempts to shut down all discussion betrays which side is exhibiting intolerance.

An Ever-Worsening Downward Spiral

There was a day when truth, decency, and civility occupied the public forum. But many people today no longer find within themselves the ability to negotiate the most trivial disagreements. We see evidence of this all over social media, where people vent their opinions with a lot of heat and very little light. Even on news programs, when guests are invited to share their perspectives, interviews frequently descend into a shouting match. In the absence of reason, character, and truth, chaos prevails.

On the one hand, we are assaulted by a radical worldview that asserts everyone has a right to do something at the expense of others. This attitude has fueled a ruthless kind of morality that is permissive and uninhibited. But as this individualism asserts itself more and more, the freedoms of others are being denied.

On the other hand, a proliferation of media that extols indecency and immorality has turned the bizarre into the normal. Moral relativism has reached a point where society no longer has any sense of a moral compass at all. We live in an "anything goes" society.

America's moral locomotive is running on the inertia of previous generations that respected the Bible, if not believed it. There was in this nation what Francis Schaeffer called a "Christian consensus": a belief that there are absolutes, that morality is more than just a matter of personal opinion and convenience. There was a commitment to values that grew out of a Judeo-Christian view of the world. But once the Bible is rejected, ungodly values are allowed to come to their natural conclusion in morality, law, and politics.

Needless to say, we who are Christians are concerned. We're feeling overwhelmed as we see so many cultural issues tear our country apart. Diversity, race, gender, social justice, free speech, and more—all have gotten so far out of hand that we wonder how we can bring a voice of reason to the table.

The great temptation for Christians is to fight this battle on cultural ground rather than spiritual. The tendency is to focus on cultural reform rather than spiritual. Because the cultural issues are so vivid and we agree that something needs to be done, we're inclined to look for solutions that end up being inadequate because they don't address the point from which all cultural issues emanate: the heart.

It is the transformation of the heart that
leads to the transformation of life.

Our battle is not against two competing moral systems; our battle is against two competing Gods. We cannot expect to persuade non-Christians to grasp the rightness or wrongness of various issues based on the issues themselves. Instead, we must proclaim the truth that made the church grow through the centuries: the fact that we are all sinners already suffering under the righteous judgment of God. We have a great deal of educating to do in a culture where only a tiny fraction of people even believe that sin is a violation of God's will.

I've learned that a defense of Christian morality, no matter how reasonable, will never change the minds of those who are determined to follow their own ways. The fact is, people act on the basis of what pleases them ("If it feels good, do it") and not on the basis of rational considerations. I have had to repeatedly learn that it is the transformation of the heart that leads to the transformation of life. That is the lesson we must adhere to if we desire to see real change take place in society.

God's answer goes to the very heart of our moral crisis: First, through faith in Christ we are acquitted, declared righteous by God Himself. And second, there is an actual transformation of the heart: "If any man is in Christ, he is a new creature; the old things passed away; behold, new things have come" (2 Corinthians 5:17). Through Christ, our relationship with God is rectified and we are eternally His.

Debating cultural issues cannot raise the dead or give sight to the blind. Moral reforms cannot take a heart of stone and turn it into a heart of flesh. We cannot do through the ballot box and social media what God is able to do through the proclamation of His message. Bringing about positive cultural change and moral reform is not enough when God commands moral transformation. God's agenda is greater, more urgent, and has eternal repercussions.

For some, the temptation to reclaim culture in the name of Christianity is irresistible. We must not fall for this temptation. Instead, we must recover the biblical doctrine of humanity's inability to do anything that pleases God. We must look upon cultural or legal victories for what they are: Band-Aids that serve as temporary patches. What's really needed is a transformation of people's hearts.

Not Reformation, but Transformation

Only with the fervency of Christ's love burning within our hearts and the gospel message can we ever hope to change culture. To opt for political or cultural transformation is like trying to push a train in our own strength. We need to kindle the fire in the engine.

What is God saying to us? We can best clean up the world by cleaning up the church. Paul had nothing to say to the pagan culture of his day except that unbelievers should repent. There was little use telling them that they should reform themselves. He knew that the problem ran much deeper—it was not a matter of reformation, but transformation.

How can we expect the citizens of the city of man to live according to the dictates of the city of God unless they have become members of that kingdom? As long as they are members of the kingdom of darkness, that darkness will appear as light to them. Perhaps nowhere is this more clearly seen than in the killing of preborn infants. Once upon a time many of us believed that we could rationally persuade the world of the error of abortion. If only we could show them that medically, philosophically, and logically the abortion of a preborn infant was infanticide.

Although a few have listened with an open mind and have changed their opinion, the vast majority of those who call themselves pro-choice have chosen to ignore the evidence and plunge ahead, advocating abortion at any time for any reason. Clearly this is a position based not on reason but on the deeply cherished convictions that people should be free to engage in immorality without having to accept the consequences of having a child, or that a woman should not have to bear the child if it's going to ruin her lifestyle. To those who blindly equate freedom for women as the right to kill the unborn infant, no argument will persuade them otherwise.

Jesus' weapon for bringing about
change was the gospel.

I'm sure you have met people, as I have, who were on the front lines of the pro-abortion debate but became Christians and changed their view to become pro-life. Or perhaps you know individuals who were formerly in a same-sex relationship, received Jesus as Savior and Lord, and have gone on to minister the grace of Christ to those around them. And these transformations happened not because of persuasive arguments, but rather, a change of heart.

I'm not suggesting that we stop presenting the Christian worldview on the many cultural issues that are dividing people today. But our results will be limited if that's all we do. Remember, the human mind is able to rationalize anything that the human heart desires to do.

Jesus' weapon for bringing about change was the gospel, not cultural or political battles. The same should be true for us, because only a change of heart will bring about a change of mind.

Only God's light can conquer the darkness.

PART 3

Preparing Ourselves to Engage with Culture

Preparing Ourselves to Engage with Culture

When it comes to publicly testifying for Jesus in today's hostile climate, it's more imperative than ever that we look at our own lives to make sure we are spiritually prepared for the task that is before us. As I said in the book *We Will Not Be Silenced*, it is easy for the gospel to get lost in a social justice-driven world. From a personal standpoint, are we ready to commit ourselves to saying what the world needs to hear? Have we equipped ourselves adequately?

With that in mind, I've included five short studies[1] on what Scripture has to say about being prepared for the battle that is before us. These studies take a closer look at the essentials for being an effective witness. As we speak God's truth and proclaim Christ, we need to be marked by

- discernment
- courage
- character
- prayer
- the gospel

At the end of each study are some brief questions designed to help you think carefully about how you can apply that essential in your life and interactions with others.

Discernment

Hebrews 5:14—*Solid food is for the mature, for those who have their powers of discernment trained by constant practice to distinguish good from evil.*

Proverbs 3:5-7—*Trust in the LORD with all your heart, and do not lean on your own understanding. In all your ways acknowledge him, and he will make straight your paths. Be not wise in your own eyes; fear the LORD, and turn away from evil.*

Discernment is the ability to make a choice based on a biblical standard that honors God and edifies and benefits us and the people around us. Unfortunately, many Christians derive their standards of conduct from the culture that surrounds them. The ways they speak and act, and the ways they view cultural issues, are influenced by society. They say and do whatever feels comfortable and imitate what others are doing without asking these basic questions: What does God say about this? What is His standard? They forget that we, as God's children, are called to a higher standard, lifestyle, and worldview that is very different from that of the people around us.

The influence and pressure from our self-centered, social justice-driven society affects pretty much everything in life. We must be diligent and use discernment to help protect ourselves in as many ways as possible from both the subtle and flagrant faulty thinking that permeates the world around us. We need to be ready to say no to people and opinions that conflict with a biblical standard.

We need to make a focused and determined effort to shield ourselves from anything that seeks to discourage, demoralize, and deceive us. We must pay attention to the instruction in 1 John 2:15-17, which says,

Do not love the world or the things in the world. If anyone loves the world, the love of the Father is not in him. For all that is in the world—the desires of the flesh and the desires of the eyes and the pride of life—is not from the Father but is from the world. And the world is passing away along with its desires, but whoever does the will of God abides forever.

In that passage, the apostle John warns us about three things. The first is "the desires of the flesh"—that is, anything that appeals to our fallen human nature and stands in opposition to God. The second is "the desires of the eyes," which refers to being drawn to what looks attractive and appealing from a worldly standpoint. The third is "the pride of life," which can be defined as self-love and absorption. To love the world is, at root, to worship the goddess of self—that is, our tendency to satisfy legitimate desires in the wrong way. Simply put, when sin or worldly ways of thinking have control over us, we render ourselves ineffective for God's work.

Why is the love of the world so serious? Because if we lower the standards, if we accommodate what the world says to feel better about itself, and most importantly, if we allow sin a foothold in our lives—even in our way of thinking—we not only love what God hates, we love what put Jesus on the cross. It is only as we resist sin and pursue personal purity that we will be able to survive the cultural pressures all around us.

If we want to become discerning and useful Christians in a corrupt culture, we must constantly ask ourselves: Would Jesus approve of this? Will this compromise how unbelievers view me as a Christian? Does this way of thinking line up with what Scripture teaches?

Discerning Christians will take heed of this warning: "Look carefully then how you walk, not as unwise but as wise, making the best use of the time, because the days are evil" (Ephesians 5:15-16). Let us ask ourselves some hard questions: Are we walking as those who are wise? Is our use of time making us a better person? Has it improved our character? Are we in the place we need to be to have a right influence on others, instead of letting them influence us? To walk as those who are wise includes spending time reading our Bible, praying, and becoming involved in the lives of others in ways that benefit them.

Someday we'll want to hear our Lord say, "Well done, good servant!" (Luke 19:17). Each of us must make a decision of conscience: From what worldly influences does the Lord want to free me? What am I embracing that is damaging my devotion and affection for God and my commitment to living out my faith?

As Christians—as those who bear light in the midst of a dark world—our greatest need is to live a righteous life before the watchful eyes of others. Without discernment, our lives will become saturated with the things that hinder our effectiveness as believers.

Taking God's Word to Heart

1. How would you define discernment as it pertains to your beliefs and actions? How do you determine what is clearly right and what is clearly wrong?

2. Give examples of how our values are often derived from contemporary culture rather than from the Bible.

3. What are some ways we can protect ourselves from the evil influences of society?

4. Based on 1 John 2:15-17, why is a love of the world so serious?

5. How can we do a better job of "making the best use of the time" in these difficult and evil days?

Courage

Joshua 1:7-8—*Only be strong and very courageous, being careful to do according to all the law that Moses my servant commanded you. Do not turn from it to the right or to the left, that you may have good success wherever you go. This Book of the Law shall not depart from your mouth, but you shall meditate on it day and night, so that you may be careful to do according to all that is written in it. For then you will make your way prosperous, and then you will have good success.*

When God gave Joshua the command to be "very courageous," Joshua was about to lead his troops into a huge battle. You can imagine the fear and apprehension of any military commander on the eve of conflict, when he is only too aware that some of his men might be killed, and conceivably, the war might go against him. In other words, he could lose. Moses was dead, and the young Joshua had to face the reality of the formidable city of Jericho on his own. This command to be courageous was accompanied with this promise: "The LORD your God is with you wherever you go" (Joshua 1:9). That is, courage was not to be found within himself but by looking beyond himself, depending on the help of his own invisible Commander.

We as believers never have to face the harsh realities of life on our own. Here is God's personal promise to us: "I will never leave you nor forsake you" (Hebrews 13:5). God walks with us on good days and bad. No matter how difficult the battle, God is there with us.

Truth be told, it is one thing to know these promises and quite another to be comforted by them. There are a couple reasons we are tempted to lack courage even though the Lord is with us. One is because we know that the promise of God's presence does not guarantee we will be free of trouble. Christians through the ages have faced every difficulty or crisis imaginable.

Another reason we're tempted to lack courage is that the assurance of God's presence does not do away with our personal struggles with temptation, sin, and regrets. These disappointments befall us all. We should be encouraged to remember that even Jesus, whose trust in the Father never wavered, cringed during His prayer in Gethsemane as He anticipated the horror that awaited Him.

How, then, do we apply these promises despite the fact we have no assurance we will be delivered from what we fear? The answer is twofold: First, we know that God can take even the worst situations in our lives and work them out for our good. We are convinced that He has a purpose in our trials that lies beyond the human eye. Yes, He has higher purposes that we can only dimly see in this life. So when we are not delivered from that which gives us fear, we need to remember God is allowing it for our good and His glory.

Second, we are assured that even struggles and doubts do not separate us from God's love and care. In moments when we are weak, God is still with us, directing, providing for, and comforting us. Even when we lack faith, He is faithful. We must remember we live by promises, not explanations.

The night Joshua was to attack Jericho, he was given a vision, a divine apparition while on a stroll around the city, thinking and planning how he would defeat it. A man appeared in the darkness (we have reason to believe this was a pre-incarnate visitation of Christ). Joshua was terrified. Thinking the man might be an enemy combatant from Jericho, he asked, "Are you for us, or for our adversaries?" And he said, "No; but I am the commander of the army of the LORD. Now I have come" (Joshua 5:13-14).

Yes, this was the Lord saying, in effect, "I have not come to take sides; I have come to take over!" And that, ultimately, is the answer for those of us who lack courage in the midst of the battles we face: Jesus is not with us merely to help us; rather, He stands ready to fight for us, if only we will trust Him and let Him take charge.

On the tomb of Lord Lawrence in Westminster Abbey are the dates of his birth and death, along with an inscription that includes this statement:

> He feared Man so little,
> because he feared God so much.

Yes, if we fear God, we need fear nothing else.

With such confidence, like Joshua, we can walk into the unknown night with courage.

Taking God's Word to Heart

1. In the midst of great danger, Joshua stood strong, trusting what God had told him. Today, we as believers can embrace the written Word of God. Share some promises from God's Word that provide you with strength in the difficult situations you face with regard to living in a hostile world.

2. "I will never leave you nor forsake you" (Hebrews 13:5) is one of the great promises of Scripture. What are some ways you can effectively apply the truths of this promise to your life of faith, particularly in relation to taking a stand on cultural issues?

3. For what reasons might we, as Christians, be tempted to lack the courage to persevere, even though we know God is with us? How can you resolve such fears when you encounter them?

4. How can we reconcile the truth of God's presence in our lives with the reality that we as Christians can experience great difficulty when we assert biblical truth and share our convictions with others?

5. Consider the statement, "We live by promises, not explanations." How should that affect the way we perceive our interactions with unbelievers in today's secular culture?

Character

Psalm 15:1-2—O Lᴏʀᴅ, *who shall sojourn in your tent?*
Who shall dwell on your holy hill? He who walks blamelessly
and does what is right and speaks truth in his heart.

Philippians 2:14-15—*Do all things without grumbling or disputing,*
that you may be blameless and innocent,
children of God without blemish in the midst of a crooked and twisted generation,
among whom you shine as lights in the world..

D L. Moody said quite accurately that character is what a man is in the dark. Unfortunately, people today find it difficult to distinguish character from reputation. In our careless generation, only one's reputation seems to matter. But our character is more important than our reputation. Others can damage your reputation, but they cannot damage your character.

Yale law professor Stephen Carter defines character (he calls it integrity) as something very specific, and it requires three steps: (1) *discerning* what is right and wrong; (2) *acting* on what you have discerned, even at personal cost; and (3) *saying openly* that you are acting on your understanding of right from wrong.[1] In other words, a person of character should not be ashamed that he or she is living with deeply held convictions. The more public we are about our commitment to integrity, the more motivated we will be to live by our standards.

Psalm 15 asks and answers these questions: "O Lᴏʀᴅ, who shall sojourn in your tent? Who shall dwell on your holy hill?" (verse 1). Then what follows is a description of the man whom God receives, the one who is allowed to scale the hill of the Lord and be pleasing to Him.

First, such a person speaks the truth: "He who walks blamelessly and does what is right and speaks truth in his heart" (verse 2). He speaks the truth no matter what—even when it puts him at risk for criticism or condemnation.

Second, the person of integrity speaks honorably to other people; he is the one "who does not slander with his tongue and does no evil to his neighbor, nor takes up a reproach against his friend" (verse 3). No matter how much he disagrees with someone or wants to strike back with strong words, he is gracious. His words of conviction are spoken with compassion.

This is the kind of character God calls us to have. Why is this so important? In the New Testament, the apostle Paul connects character with our witness for Christ. He urges us to be "blameless and innocent, children of God without blemish in the midst of a crooked and twisted generation, among whom you shine as lights in the world" (Philippians 2:15).

Without character, our witness is muted or even destroyed.

Character is fragile. It is like a vase on a mantel that, after it falls to the floor, shatters, and is glued back together again, still evidences some hairline cracks showing where it was damaged. That is why, as you accept the challenge of representing Christ to a watching world, you should guard your integrity. Your character is your most precious possession. With it, people might be willing to listen to you. But without it, they won't.

Good character is a virtue that makes people more willing to consider what you have to say.

Taking God's Word to Heart

1. How do you define character? Why is character important to you? Explain how Psalm 15:1-2 defines character.

2. Discuss the characteristics of a person with integrity. What happens to our integrity when we fail to align our thoughts, words, and actions with the truth?

3. Why is personal character important to our witness for Christ?

4. Are you willing to preserve your integrity no matter what the cost? Recall an instance in which you paid a cost for maintaining good character.

5. Your character is a fragile possession. What steps do you take to guard your character so that you can be blameless before others?

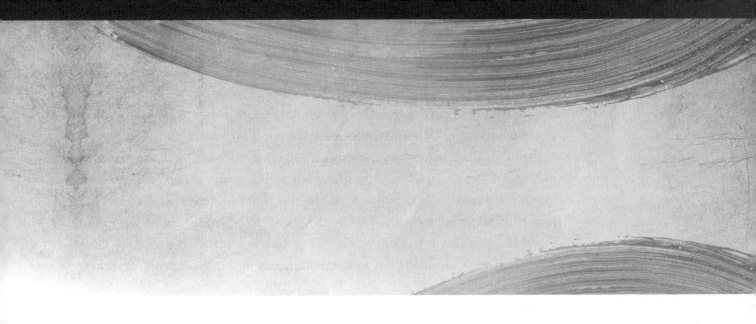

Prayer

Mark 1:35—*Rising very early in the morning, while it was still dark, he departed and went out to a desolate place, and there he prayed.*

Ephesians 6:18—*[Be] praying at all times in the Spirit, with all prayer and supplication. To that end, keep alert with all perseverance, making supplication for all the saints.*

When I asked Jim Cymbala, of the Brooklyn Tabernacle in New York, why people stood outside the door of his church on a Tuesday evening waiting for the doors to open so they would be among the first to find a seat for the weekly prayer meeting, he answered simply, "Your church would also be filled every week for prayer meeting if the people believed that God answered prayer...and that things would be different after they prayed."

How simple but true! Every Christian would be eager to pray if he or she truly believed that God answered prayer and that prayer changes circumstances. However, truth be told, some people who have seen their prayers left unanswered have become cynical and think that prayer doesn't do much. Moreover, many believers spend only a few minutes in prayer each day, usually asking God for help with routine, everyday requests.

How can we break such disinterest in prayer? And restore prayer to its proper place in our lives—especially when it comes to the more momentous requests we might have? First, we must grapple with the widespread assumption that the sovereignty of God is an impediment to prayer. The argument goes like this: Because God has a certain plan that He intends to carry out, and because He has limitless power to do so, how can my prayer possibly affect His will? Conclusion: Whatever will be will be.

Interestingly, Jesus taught that God's sovereignty was not a *hindrance* to prayer, but rather a *basis* for prayer. He told the disciples that they should not become repetitious like the heathen, who thought they would be heard because of their many words. Then Jesus taught the disciples how to pray by giving what is commonly known as the Lord's Prayer (see Matthew 6:5-14). Note that the fact our heavenly Father has prior knowledge of all events should not discourage us from praying, but give us confidence as we pray!

Don't let the puzzle of God's sovereignty and what is commonly called our free will be a hindrance to your prayers. In fact, these things should *motivate* us to ask great things of God.

Second, it is clear from Scripture that God wants us to move beyond our litany of routine requests to develop a relationship with Him. If we see the first purpose of prayer as getting our petitions answered, we are likely to end up like a whiny child whose attitude toward his father depends entirely on whether he gets what he wants when he wants it. We will think that one day God is kind because He answers a prayer, and the next day He is indifferent because we don't get what we want. Given that focus, no wonder we lack enthusiasm for prayer!

Now, it is true that God can do whatever He wants whether we pray or not. So it stands to reason that the first purpose of prayer is *not* to get our requests answered, as such. The reason God permits us to experience so many needs is that they are what nudge us into His presence. And once we are there, our focus shifts and we realize we need God's presence more than we need the answers we seek. If we draw near to God because we are seeking Him, we will discover that the first purpose of prayer will always be achieved whether or not we get the answer we want.

This kind of praying is driven by praise and thanksgiving; it is a kind of prayer that submits to God and finds delight in being in His presence. This changes prayer from being a boring or seemingly irrelevant experience and turns it into a time of intimate fellowship with our heavenly Father. This kind of praying seeks the Lord Himself, not just His answers to our lists of requests.

Jesus often spent whole nights in prayer and yet this did not spare Him the trauma of Gethsemane and the painful humiliation of the cross. It is clear that for Him, fellowship with the Father was His highest priority. He knew that if He was intimately connected with His Father, He could endure whatever lay ahead.

Ironically, we need fellowship with God more than we need help in the midst of difficult situations. God's first priority is not to change our circumstances, but to change us. This is particularly relevant when it comes to persevering in the midst of the cultural battles raging in today's world.

Third, we must realize that once God has been put in His rightful place in our prayer life, praying for His will to be done—no matter what it might be—becomes easier and more doable. Now we are able to approach Him with an attitude of submission; we can even "hear His voice" not in words to be sure, but deep within there is a peace that profoundly accepts whatever God gives us. And, no matter what happens, we know God has permitted it and is with us. This is a tremendous assurance to have in the face of the tremendous opposition we face in today's society.

When the apostle Paul said we should pray "in the Spirit" (Ephesians 6:18), he was referring to a connection with God that not only acknowledges His sovereignty but also recognizes that what God does *in* us is often more important than what God does *through* us, or what He does outside of us.

It is from this kind of relationship that petitions flow with a right attitude from our hearts to God. Only on the strength of the intimacy of our relationship with God can we give our requests to Him and be at peace. Then our hearts are guarded because our relationship with God remains firm regardless of the outcome of our prayer requests.

To accept the invitation to meet with God is our highest privilege. When we move from requests to relationship, we enter into the heart of what God had in mind when we were told to pray continuously without fainting. This, in turn, has a very real impact on our ability to stand strong in the face of today's cultural headwinds.

Remember, desperation leads us to prayer…and prayer leads us to the heart of God.

Taking God's Word to Heart

1. How important is prayer to your life of faith? How much time do you spend seeking God in prayer?

2. Read again the comments about God's sovereignty. How does God's control of all things relate to our prayer life? How is it a basis for our prayers?

3. What should be our first purpose in prayer? What should be our focus during prayer?

4. What was Jesus' approach to prayer as we see it in the Gospels? What characterized His prayers? What were His priorities?

5. Why is the quality of our relationship with God so important to our prayer life? How do you think this helps us as we live courageously in a culture that is hostile to Christianity?

The Gospel

Matthew 5:14,16—*You are the light of the world…let your light shine before others, that they may see your good works and give glory to your Father who is in heaven.*

1 Peter 3:15—*In your hearts honor Christ the Lord as holy, always being prepared to make a defense to anyone who asks you for a reason for the hope that is in you; yet do it with gentleness and respect.*

We are living at a time of increased animosity toward Christians. Quite apart from whether we deserve it or not, we are viewed as narrow-minded, judgmental, and bigoted.

How do we let our light shine in a world where people are comfortable in their moral and spiritual darkness? We deeply believe that we have a great opportunity to impact our culture, and more importantly, to change the spiritual direction of those who are within our sphere of influence. We have the privilege of living at a time when millions of seekers are trying to find their way amid a blizzard of cultural controversy. If we are sensitive to human needs, we will soon learn that many people are seeking answers, and that may bring us the privilege of helping them on their spiritual journey.

Many today cannot tolerate the idea that God alone possesses the truth and that their concepts of equality and justice don't line up with His. They take offense at the Christian worldview of the cultural issues that are causing so much strife today.

How do we witness to people who have a hostile mindset?

First, people must actually see the light. We must avoid being obnoxious, but at the same time we must resist the temptation to keep our mouths shut. One excellent way to share our faith is by asking questions, by finding out where others are on their spiritual journey. We do what we can to invite discussion, and we take the time to listen to what others are thinking about the Bible, the Christian worldview, and Jesus in particular.

How is this done? Here are some questions you can use to begin or carry on a conversation:

- How did you arrive at the views you presently hold?
- Are you curious about what Jesus' views might be on this issue?
- Have you ever considered what the Bible says about this issue?
- What has been your experience, if any, with Christianity?
- Would you mind if I were to share with you something that someone once shared with me that changed my life?
- I'd love to pray for you. Do you have anything you'd like me to pray about over the next couple of weeks?

If you look at the Gospels, you'll notice that Jesus carried on dialogue with people around Him by asking questions. A further step you can take is to give a friend or colleague a book to read, saying, "I think you'll enjoy reading this. Could we meet again to discuss it in a few weeks?" The book itself might or might not be gospel-centered, but your purpose is to open up opportunities for dialogue. Other books can follow later.

We must also learn, as best we can, how to defend the Christian worldview and our faith. Many Christians feel intimidated about sharing their faith because they think they need to know all the answers before getting into a discussion. But in today's cultural climate, being a good listener is more important than being a good talker. People want to be heard. And listening to what they say and feel is the first step to building a bridge that leads to their hearts.

What should you do if you encounter hostility? Befriend the person and ask why he or she is so angry toward or turned off by Christianity or a biblical worldview. Many people have, humanly speaking, good reason to regard Christians with skepticism and distrust. True friendship is still the best means of evangelism. One reason the early church was so successful is that the early believers practiced the art of hospitality. Their kindness reached the world.

Finally, and perhaps most important of all, we ourselves must live in the light. Think of how hollow our witness is when we are not living authentically—that is, living with the heart of a servant, and with integrity. Notice that Jesus said those who live in darkness should see our good works and glorify the Father who is in heaven (Matthew 5:16). Good deeds back up our good words and give credibility to the light.

We also must remember that only God can open the human heart and draw sinners to Himself. Our responsibility is to share the message; it is God's responsibility to supply the enablement to respond to the knowledge that has been imparted. As Jesus put it, "No one can come to me unless the Father who sent me draws him. And I will raise him up on the last day" (John 6:44).

God will not hold us accountable if others do not believe the gospel; rather, He will hold us accountable if we do not share the gospel. Our responsibility is to sow the seed, and His responsibility is to prepare the soil of the human heart to receive it. Only He can grant the faith needed to believe the gospel.

Speaking to others about Christ with courage and love is the great need of the hour!

Taking God's Word to Heart

1. What reasons might people have for wanting to know the biblical viewpoint on a cultural issue?

2. How do we impact a lost world that is too comfortable in their spiritual darkness? How can we get the attention of a culture that does not generally respect Christians or the gospel?

3. One way to engage the lost is by asking them questions. Review the questions listed on page 154. What are some other questions you can use in your encounters with others?

4. Another key aspect of witnessing to the lost is being able to defend your Christian beliefs. Are you able to give a reason for your faith? What are among the things you can say?

5. It's vital for the lost to see authentic Christianity in action, for that serves as a living testimony in the midst of our dark culture. What happens when we shine our light in the darkness?

PART 4

Answering the Questions
People Are Asking

Answering the Questions
People Are Asking

In the months after the book *We Will Not Be Silenced* was published, I was invited to do many interviews. The book generated a lot of discussions and questions people had about what is going on in America today.

Below is a representative cross-section of the questions asked, with the answers combining responses that were given in different interviews. My hope is that you'll find this information to be a useful supplement to what was offered in the book and this workbook.

Aren't we as Christians to try to reclaim the culture?
Isn't that part of our obligation as Christian citizens?

It's true that in Romans 13:1, the apostle Paul urges all believers to "be subject to the governing authorities." We're to live in obedience to civil authorities. And it's true that we're to be a positive influence to those around us, to be the salt of the earth and the light of the world (Matthew 5:13-14).

But being good citizens who seek to bring about change through voting for the right government officials and laws does not equal taking back culture. Though we are called to live as examples, and while God may call certain people to be involved in politics in some way or other, note that Scripture never encourages believers to take back the culture or attempt to replace a secular government with a Christian one.

Christ Himself never advocated political reform. His life and ministry were carried out under a government that was thoroughly secular. When asked about whether it was lawful to pay taxes to Caesar, He said, "Render to Caesar the things that are Caesar's, and to God the things that are God's" (Mark 12:17). Given the opportunity to reject or condemn an ungodly government's authority over God's chosen people, He didn't.

When a band of soldiers came to arrest Jesus prior to His crucifixion, Peter pulled out his sword to fight back. What was Jesus' response? He told Peter to put away the sword (John 18:11). Jesus was not an insurrectionist; He did not resist arrest, the unjust trials carried out against Him, nor the crucifixion itself, which was the greatest injustice in all history.

What Scripture *does* call us to do is to share the gospel so that people's hearts and lives may be transformed. Our weapon for bringing about change is the good news, not political or moral battles. We cannot expect people to have a change of mind before they have a change of heart.

I don't like to be pessimistic, but personally, I believe today's culture is beyond the point of being able to be reclaimed. We've crossed too many boundaries; so much of what is unbiblical has become the norm.

In line with Christ's admonishment for us to strengthen what remains, our greatest concern right now should be to make sure the church doesn't succumb to the culture. That's why I wrote *We Will Not Be Silenced*. In today's world, all too often we see the church buying into the culture instead of standing against it. Another problem is that many Christians don't know how to respond to the controversial social issues swirling all around us in a way that balances both compassion and conviction.

Today's Christian is caught in a difficult dilemma. We want to show love to the world, yet we also need to hold fast to truth and live in holiness. While we should be welcoming to those with whom we disagree, that doesn't mean we need to be affirming of them.

Our responsibility is to proclaim the Savior so that the world may realize He is their only hope. Let us be faithful for His glory as we bring as many people as possible with us as we travel the narrow road.

What is the difference between the classic Marxism that Russia and China are known for and the cultural Marxism in America today?

As stated in *We Will Not Be Silenced*, Karl Marx's view was that natural law and Judeo-Christian values breed inequality and feed on greed and systemic oppression. All of this—including the traditional family structure—had to be dismantled before equality and justice (as Marx interpreted them) could be achieved. His solution was for the rejection of Judeo-Christian values and for the state to control all wealth so that it could be distributed evenly to everyone. This included taking over all means of producing goods and resources.

Marx called for the oppressed—or victims—to rise up in a revolution, destabilize the existing order, and replace it with a new kind of government control and Marxist values. In Russia, this was accomplished through violent uprisings in which millions of people were killed.

Today's cultural Marxists advocate the same values Marx did and pursue the same goals of equality and justice, but they are doing so not on battlefields. Instead, they are attempting to bring about change through gradual transformation. The means they are using to accomplish this are the education system, the media, the political process, and the legal system. Cultural Marxism is attractively packaged as offering hope, change, income equality, racial harmony, and justice—all on the basis of secular values and not biblical ones.

Cultural Marxists have a utopian dream, and it is endeavoring to influence society not with guns, as done with classical Marxism, but by capturing people's hearts and minds. However, as we saw happen in the summer of 2020 (and this will likely continue in the days ahead), some advocates of cultural Marxism have resorted to violent protests and burning buildings to further their agenda.

What is the difference between biblical justice and social justice?

The Bible is filled with references to the need for justice. Scripture talks about the necessity of justice when it comes to the law. And the form of justice we usually think about is taking care of and identifying with those who need help and cannot speak for themselves. We are to watch over and stand up for those who are poor or oppressed. All that is part of biblical justice.

Social justice, however, promotes a different way of thinking. It's rooted in the cultural Marxist view of equality, which means that all people are to be treated as equals. This is why social justice insists on the affirmation of same-sex relationships and transgenderism. The goal in social justice is to equalize everything and to eradicate distinctions, even if they are legitimate.

Scripture teaches that men and women have equal value before God yet different roles He has designed for them. God has instructed us on sexual issues—on what is right and what is wrong. The Bible recognizes people are gifted differently, as in the case when one man was entrusted with ten talents, another with five, and so on. Though we are all made in the image of God, we have differences, and we shouldn't attempt to obliterate them in the way cultural Marxism does.

As believers, we should absolutely do what we can to help those in need and to treat people fairly. That's our obligation. But that is entirely different from the kind of equality that social justice attempts to bring about by insisting on, for example, income equality that doesn't take into consideration a person's skill levels, abilities, and experience.

Why are cultural Marxists so eager to rewrite history?

A key part of controlling the future is changing the past. Part of ushering in a different way of government is attacking the past as unworthy of being preserved. Cultural Marxists are using a broad brush to paint everything about the past as being wrong and blaming the past for today's problems. By casting the past in an entirely negative light, they justify the changes they want to make. Tearing down statues and changing the names of buildings are two symbolic yet significant ways they've done that.

The problem with this approach is that it throws out the good along with the bad. There's no question that America's past has some dark episodes in it. But the solution isn't to eradicate it or to deny those episodes existed. We learn from our mistakes, and we move forward with our eyes open, determined not to return to that which was wrong yet continue building on everything that we've done right. We have made progress, and there is more we can do to make things better, but it doesn't require destroying the country and starting all over.

One example of the way history is being rewritten by cultural Marxists is they're saying it was slavery that made America what it is. The way they argue this almost creates the impression that America invented slavery. But the US ended slavery more than 150 years ago, and there are still some 40 million slaves in the world today—mostly in Africa and India.

While slavery existed in America, it wasn't what made America the prosperous and capitalistic nation that it is today. Slavery was already being outlawed in a number of the northern states by the late 1700s, and this trend continued well before the Civil War. Historians tell us that the backbone of America's success was the industrial revolution, which took place largely in the non-slave states. The majority of the industries contributing to prosperity in the US were in non-slave states. The slave-based businesses in the South did not contribute as much to America's economy as cultural Marxists claim. But for cultural Marxists to get the change they want, they need to tear down all of America so they can rebuild it according to their vision.

Can Critical Race Theory help bring about more racial reconciliation?

While we as Christians should always support efforts toward racial reconciliation, we need to recognize that Critical Race Theory (CRT) does not do that. CRT does what cultural Marxism does—it categorizes people in different classes and instigates strife between those classes. White people are labelled oppressors, and African Americans are the oppressed. CRT teaches that white people, by default, are guilty of racism and inequality. CRT judges people on the basis of their skin color. That's what racism, as traditionally defined, does—it stereotypes and makes assumptions about people based on their race and no other factors.

One example of the way CRT works is that a wealthy African American would not be considered a person of privilege solely because he or she is black. Yet a poor white person is said to be a privileged oppressor merely because he or she is white. A person's background, economic status, education level, and most importantly, character qualities are not taken into consideration when defining whether he or she is privileged or a victim. Rather, CRT makes judgments on the basis of skin color.

That's different from what Martin Luther King Jr. advocated. He urged that we judge one another not by the color of our skin, but by the content of our character. CRT also doesn't line up with what Scripture says about how we should treat people. There is no scriptural support at all for what CRT teaches about race issues.

Christianity does not blame the world's problems on the fact certain classes of people are oppressors or oppressed. Nor does it nurture perpetual conflict between those classes the way cultural Marxism does. Rather, it says we all have a common problem: We are sinners. We all need the Lord. We have a sin problem rather than a skin problem—it is sin that is the true source of race problems. When we receive Christ as our Savior and Lord, no matter what our race, we all have Christ living in us. Because of the indwelling Holy Spirit, we possess unity in Christ, and we are able to exhibit Christlike character. It is in Christ alone that we are able to find the solutions to humanity's problems. Cultural Marxism rejects all that.

Because of the cross, we can know unity in the midst of diversity. The privileged can ask how they can help the underprivileged. We are all able to see each other as equals, and to bring about real justice as God defines it.

Why are cultural Marxism and freedom of speech at odds with each other?

Cultural Marxism says that those who are oppressors—those who are privileged—have no right to speak. Only the oppressed should be allowed to speak.

Marxist thinking also says that if you agree with capitalism, then you are an oppressor, and therefore, you have no right to speak. Given that view of capitalism, Marxism teaches that as long as freedom of speech is available to people, then capitalists will win the argument. You'll never be able to have a Marxist state until capitalism is eradicated.

What's ironic about all this is that the reason Marxists are able to present their views in the public forum is because of freedom of speech. They are taking advantage of this freedom for themselves in their attempt to shut it down for everyone else. They don't want any competing voices.

Cultural Marxists also know that by being aggressively vocal and intimidating people, they are creating an atmosphere of fear that causes anyone who disagrees with them to stay silent. We as Christians experience this fear as well. We're reluctant to say anything because we're afraid that we might be attacked in some way for daring to speak up. That's exactly what the secular leftists want. Even though the US still has freedom of speech, the climate of fear that has been created by cultural Marxists has led people to silence and censor themselves.

What exactly is propaganda, and why should we be so alert to it?

In *We Will Not Be Silenced*, I define propaganda as a message that attempts to change people's perception of reality so that even when they are confronted with a mountain of evidence about reality, they will not change their minds.

An example of this is the way Christians are typecast as being hateful because they disagree with same-sex relationships. Secular leftists have taken control of this discussion by changing the meanings of words and altering the facts. They say that if you don't agree with same-sex relationships, then you are hateful. Because Christians are supposed to be loving, they should be willing to accept same-sex relationships.

But the mere fact Christians disagree with something doesn't mean they hate it. And for us as believers to show love for those who are in a same-sex relationship doesn't mean we must approve of that relationship.

Recently, the board of supervisors in San Francisco has adopted the use of more sanitized terms when referring to criminals. A "convicted felon" is now called a "justice-involved person." The words "offender" and "addict" are prohibited. The purpose of all this? "The local officials say the new language will help change people's views about those who commit crimes."[2] This kind of thinking has its roots in cultural Marxism.

By redefining love, hate, tolerance, intolerance, and other such words, cultural Marxists are able to portray themselves as doing what is right and everyone else as doing what is wrong. They create a perception that doesn't square with reality. That's what propaganda does.

Why are secular leftists so determined to get at our children and sexualize them?

Cultural Marxism teaches that children belong to society, not to parents. It views the family unit as oppressive, and therefore, it is necessary to break down the family. This is why many secular educators do everything they can to distance children from their parents and indoctrinate them with core beliefs that will further their agenda. As Peter Hitchens observed in his book *The Rage Against God*, "Any ideological or revolutionary state must always alienate the young from their pre-revolutionary parents if it hopes to survive into future generations."[3]

Among the ways secular leftists accomplish this goal is through sex-education classes. They use the topics of sexuality and gender as gateways to teach the cultural Marxist view of equality that affects how we view all of society. The ultimate goals are to destroy any concept of the traditional family by attacking sacred or normal views about sex.

Because this is all done in an effort to promote the cultural Marxist definition of equality, great emphasis is placed on "seeking respect for all forms of sexuality." That explains why the sexual curriculum so actively promotes LGBTQ values.

All in the name of equality, children are taught sexual values that are aimed at destroying the family and normalizing the bizarre. Such children, once indoctrinated, go on to become the next generation of advocates programmed to carry on the core tenets of cultural Marxism.

Why do people find socialism so attractive?

The premise behind socialism is that when the government is given ownership of medical care, education, welfare, and more, it is able to equally distribute all these benefits to people for free. As the government controls the economy and prices, it takes wealth and redistributes it evenly where it is needed.

This is sold to people under the banner of equality. Everyone should have equal access to health care, a college education, retirement benefits, and so on.

Here's the problem: Because socialism insists on income equality, pay scales do not reward advanced training, hard work, or experience. Why become a medical doctor if you're not going to get paid much more than an entry-level worker? And why provide the best kind of medical care when you're required to cut corners in order to keep costs low, as required by a socialist government's policies and price controls? These are just a couple of the many ways that socialism discourages people from being creative, innovative, and motivated. Because there is no incentive to excel, and because the government determines what is to be done and how, advancement and growth are discouraged.

Socialism always focuses on equal access and distribution, and not the actual creation of wealth. Capitalism, in contrast, makes it possible for people to create wealth, which then can be used to make a wider variety of medical, educational, and vocational options available, among other things.

How is it that radical Islam and the radical left are willing to join hands in attacking America when they so greatly disagree with each other?

Both radical Islam and the radical left are committed to destroying capitalism and Christianity in America. Though they have two very different worldviews, they are allies in the same war.

Interestingly, while the ACLU is very firm about the need for separation between church and state, it says nothing about the lack of separation between mosque and state. Why the double standard? Because the ACLU—and the secular left—want to eradicate Christian influence in schools. The secular left also condemns Christians who care to voice disagreement with same-sex relationships or transgenderism yet is silent about the fact Islam also disagrees with those sexual issues.

Having said that, I want to point out that most Muslims in America are friendly, and they appreciate what the American dream makes possible for them. They want to have a safe place to raise their families, become educated, get good jobs, and contribute to society. We who are Christians should gladly reach out with a welcoming hand to the Muslims who love among us.

Why are so many people politically angry today?

There is a lot of disagreement on political and social issues today, and one reason there is so much anger out there is because people have become so devoted to a specific viewpoint they're unwilling to budge. Rather than have calm discussions in which different views are presented and an attempt is made at compromise, too many people today are determined to get their way. We live in a culture where the person who shouts the loudest is the winner.

It doesn't help that many people use social media as a means to vent their outrage. It's easy to just vent and say whatever you want to say online without facing any consequences for it. So the tone of political disagreements has become much harsher, more judgmental.

The secular left and cultural Marxists are also determined to silence their opposition. They do this by vilifying people, and intimidating them into silence. Instead of civil discussions, we now see roving gangs of rioters who protest, loot, and burn things down in order to get their way.

We Will Not Be Silenced *is dedicated to all who are willing to carry the cross of Christ. What does it mean to bear the cross?*

Sometimes people think that to "carry your cross" refers to enduring through the difficulties of life. For example, they'll say, "I have cancer, and that's my cross." Or, "I am in the middle of a difficult family situation, and that's my cross."

But when Jesus talked about bearing the cross, I believe He was referring to the troubles we face because of the fact we follow Him. It's very common for believers in other countries to be persecuted for their faith. But here in America, we've enjoyed so many freedoms, including the freedom of speech, that we have rarely found ourselves facing difficulty because of the fact we are Christians.

In our increasingly secular culture, however, that is changing. The culture is closing in on us. The days of casual Christianity are over. It's much more difficult for us to "merely get by." To live according to biblical truth puts us at odds with the world. We are much more likely to be vilified for our beliefs and our refusal to submit to culture's demands.

It is a new day in America, and we must stand for Christ. We must be willing to take the criticism and shame that may come, and to consider opposition a badge of honor.

Notes

Part 1: We Will Not Be Silenced Workbook

Lesson 2—Rewriting the Past to Control the Future

1. Alan L. Olmstead and Paul W. Rhode, as cited in Corey Lacono, "No, Slavery Did Not Make America Rich," *Foundation for Economic Education*, September 28, 2019, https://fee.org/articles/no-slavery-did-not-make-america-rich/ (emphasis added).

Lesson 4—Freedom of Speech for Me, but Not for Thee

1. Herbert Marcuse, Repressive Tolerance, https://www.marcuse.org/herbert/publications/1960s/1965-repressive-tolerance-fulltext.html.

Lesson 8—Join with Radical Islam to Destroy America

1. *Shariah: The Threat to America: Abridged* (Washington, DC: The Center for Security Policy, 2016), 40, https://www.centerforsecuritypolicy.org/2016/06/30/shariah-the-threat-to-america-abridged/.

Part 2: How Should We View Our Place in Today's Culture?

1. This material is taken and adapted from my book *Why the Cross Can Do What Politics Can't* (Eugene, OR: Harvest House Publishers, 1999), 135-156.

Part 3: Preparing Ourselves to Engage with Culture

1. These five studies, or chapters, are taken and adapted from Erwin and Rebecca Lutzer, *Life-Changing Bible Verses You Should Know* (Eugene, OR: Harvest House Publishers, 2011).

Part 4: Answering the Questions People Are Asking

1. Lukas Mikelionis, "San Francisco board rebrands 'convicted felon' as 'justice-involved person,' sanitizes other crime lingo," *Fox News*, August 22, 2019, foxnews.com/politics/san-francisco-adopts-new-language-for-criminals-turning-convicted-felon-into-justice-involved-person.

2. Peter Hitchens, *The Rage Against God* (Grand Rapids, MI: Zondervan, 2010), 139.

Other Great Books by Erwin W. Lutzer

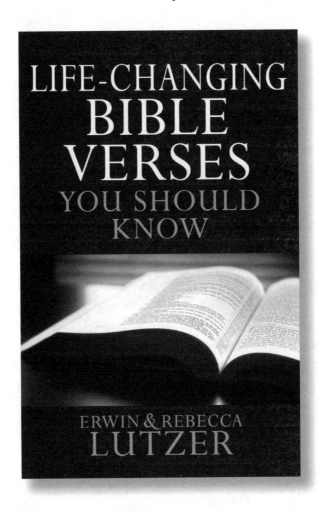

Life-Changing Bible Verses You Should Know
With Rebecca Lutzer

Do you desire to experience the life-changing power of God's Word? Do you long to hide God's Word in your heart, but don't know where to start?

In this book, Bible teacher Erwin Lutzer and his wife, Rebecca, have carefully selected more than 100 Bible verses that speak directly to the most important issues of life, and explain the very practical ways those verses can encourage and strengthen you.

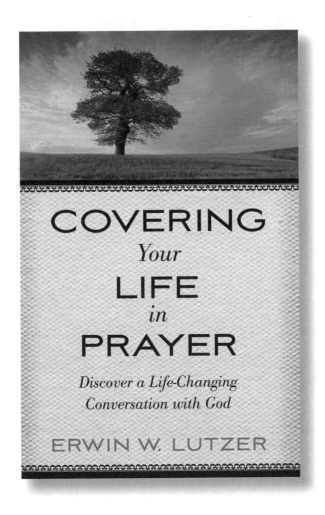

Covering Your Life in Prayer

Every Christian longs for a better and more intimate prayer life. And one of the most effective ways you can grow more powerful in prayer is to learn from the prayers of others. In this book you'll discover new ways to pray—new requests, concerns, and thanksgivings you can bring to God's throne of grace. A wonderful resource for expanding your prayer horizons and enriching your relationship with God.

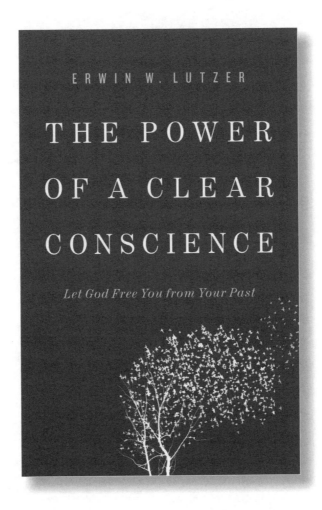

The Power of a Clear Conscience

Do you struggle with feelings of guilt about your past? Or are you bogged down by a conscience that haunts or imprisons you?

This is not how God intends for you to live. Your conscience was not created to hold you prisoner, but to guide you and point you to freedom from guilt and bad habits. Longtime pastor Erwin Lutzer shares what it means to live in the power of a clear conscience as you

- learn how to deal with guilt and replace it with joy
- discover how the truth that can hurt you can also heal you
- realize the incredible extent of God's forgiveness and love for you

You'll find yourself encouraged by the truths that no failure is permanent and no life is beyond God's power to bring about change.

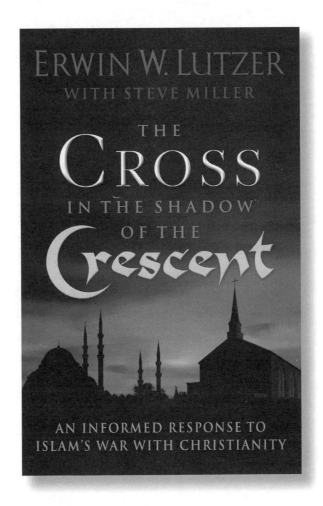

The Cross in the Shadow of the Crescent

Islam is on the rise all over the West, including in America. In this compelling book, Erwin Lutzer urges Christians to see this as both an opportunity to share the gospel and a reason for concern. Along the way, you'll find helpful answers to these questions and more:

- How does Islam's growing influence affect me personally?
- In what ways are our freedoms of speech and religion in danger?
- How can I extend Christ's love to Muslims around me?

A sensitive, responsible, and highly informative must-read!

To learn more about Harvest House books and
to read sample chapters, visit our website:

www.harvesthousepublishers.com

HARVEST HOUSE PUBLISHERS
EUGENE, OREGON